The Woman Movement

By

Ellen Key

Author of
"The Century of the Child," "Love and Marriage," etc.

Translated by

Mamah Bouton Borthwick, A.M.

With an Introduction by

Havelock Ellis

G. P. Putnam's Sons
New York and London
The Knickerbocker Press
1912

Copyright, 1912
BY
G. P. PUTNAM'S SONS

The Knickerbocker Press, New York

Printing Statement:

Due to the very old age and scarcity of this book, many of the pages may be hard to read due to the blurring of the original text, possible missing pages, missing text, dark backgrounds and other issues beyond our control.

Because this is such an important and rare work, we believe it is best to reproduce this book regardless of its original condition.

Thank you for your understanding.

By Ellen Key

The Century of the Child
The Education of the Child
Love and Marriage
The Woman Movement

Es gibt kein Vergangenes das man zurücksehnen dürfte; es gibt nur ein ewig Neues, das sich aus den erweiterten Elementen des Vergangenen gestaltet, und die echte Sehnsucht muss stets productiv sein, ein neues, besseres Erschaffen.—GOETHE.

"There is no past that we need long to return to, there is only the eternally new which is formed out of enlarged elements of the past; and our genuine longing must always be productive, for a new and better creation."

PREFACE

THE literature upon the right and the worth of woman, beginning as early as the 15th century, has in recent times increased so enormously that a complete collection would require a whole library building. In these writings are represented all classes, from tables of statistics to comic papers. Not only both sexes but almost all stages of life have contributed to it. By immersing oneself in this literature, especially in its belletristic and polemic portions, one could find rich material for the illumination of that sphere to which the publisher limited my work: the indication of the new spiritual conditions, transformations, and reciprocal results which the woman movement has effected. Historic, scientific, political, economic, juridical, sociological, and theological points of view must, therefore, be practically set aside. But even for my task, limited to the psychological sphere, time, strength, and inclination are wanting to bury myself in this literature. I must, therefore, confine myself to giving chiefly my own observations.

It is more than fifty years ago that I read *Hertha*, Sweden's first "feministic" (dealing with the woman question) novel, and listened to the numerous contentions concerning it. With ever keener personal interest I have since followed the operations of the woman movement—above all, the new psychic conditions, types, and forms of activities which the woman movement has evoked; I have also given consideration to the new possibilities and new difficulties resulting therefrom for individuals and for society.

The limited compass of this little book prevents me from substantiating my assertions by means of parallels with earlier times, comparisons which might illuminate certain spiritual transformations and new formations. My comparisons of the present with the past do not go farther back than my own memory reaches. And these touch, moreover, in what concerns the past, principally upon Swedish conditions; while my impressions of the present were gathered throughout Europe. I have considered, however, that I could summarise both in a comprehensive picture. For although the women of Sweden a generation ago possessed rights for which the women in many countries are still struggling to-day, yet the woman movement in the last decade has advanced so rapidly that the conditions have in great measure been equalised. Indeed, some of the grey-haired champions of the woman movement have seen one after another of their demands fulfilled in this new century—demands which in the fifties and sixties, in many countries even in the seventies and eighties, were publicly and privately derided even in the very person of these champions. And among peoples who even ten years ago were unaffected by the emancipation of women, for example the Chinese and the Turks, it is already progressing. It amounts to this, that even if national peculiarities in character and in laws occasion differences in the curve which the woman movement describes in the different countries, yet everywhere the movement has had the same causes, must follow the same main direction, and—sooner or later—must have the same effects.

. . . . . .

In *Hertha*, the book containing the tenets of the Swedish woman movement, the demand is made for woman's "freedom and future, and a home for her spiritual life"; the desire is expressed that women should "preserve the character of their own nature, and not be uniformly moulded, not be led by a string as if they had not a soul of their own to show them the way." There must be "vital air for woman's soul and a share in life's riches." It is to be lamented that "woman's spiritual talent must be a field that lies fallow," that the law "denies her free agency in seeking happiness." The prerogative is demanded that "woman in noble self-conscious joy shall succeed in feeling what she is able to do now and what she is capable of attaining"; that she shall be free to "aspire to the heights her youthful strength and consciousness point out to her"; that she may "be fully herself and be able to exercise an uplifting, ennobling influence upon the man" to whom she says: "All that is mine shall be thine and thereby the portion of each shall be doubled."

Even if all fields are made accessible to them, "God's law in their nature will always lead the majority of women to the home, to the intimacy of the family life, to motherhood and the duties of rearing children—but with a higher consciousness." That women shall be citizens signifies that they shall become "human beings in whom the life of the heart predominates."

This picture of the future, which has already become a reality in many respects, was sketched at a time when innumerable women were still compelled to experience that "there is no heavier burden than life's emptiness," and when it was true of every woman, "dark is her way, gloomy her future, narrow her lot."

But because that *which is*, is always considered by the masses as that which *ought to be*, "whatever is, is right," so the writer who painted the picture was called "dangerous," "a disintegrator of society," "mad," "ridiculous"! "Mademoiselle Bremer's" name possessed then quite a different intonation from that of Fredrika Bremer now; it caused strife between the sexes; it was hated by some and derided by others.

I should like to advise young women of the present time to read *Hertha;* they will thus obtain a criterion for the progress which has taken place during the last half century and also a clear view of the character of the opposition which the present desire for progress encounters.

ELLEN KEY.

October 1, 1909.

INTRODUCTION

THERE can be little doubt that at the present moment what is called the "Woman's Movement" is entering a critical period of its development. A discussion of its present problems and its present difficulties by one of the most advanced leaders in that movement thus appears at the right time and deserves our most serious attention.

The early promulgators of the Woman's Movement, a century or more ago, rightly regarded it as an extremely large and comprehensive movement affecting the whole of life. They were anxious to secure for women adequate opportunities for free human development, to the same extent that men possess such opportunities, but they laid no special stress on the abolition of any single disability or group of disabilities, whether as regards education, occupation, marriage, property, or political enfranchisement. They were people of wide and sound intelligence; they never imagined that any single isolated reform would prove a cheap panacea for all the evils they wished to correct; they looked for a slow reform along the whole line. They held that such reform would enrich and enlarge the entire field of human life, not for women only, but for the human race generally. Such, indeed, is the spirit which still inspires the wisest and most far-seeing champions of that Movement. It is only necessary to mention Olive Schreiner's *Woman and Labour*.

When, however, the era of actual practical reform began, it was obvious that a certain amount of concentration became necessary. Education was, reasonably enough, usually the first point for concentration, and gradually, without any undue friction, the education of girls was, so far as possible, raised to a level not so very different from that of boys. This first great stage in the Woman's Movement inevitably led on to the second stage, which lay in a struggle, not this time always without a certain amount of friction, to secure the entry of these now educated women to avocations and professions previously monopolised by the men who had alone been trained to fill them. This second stage is now largely completed, and at the present time there are very few vocations and professions in civilised lands, even in so conservative and slowly moving a land as England, which women are not entitled to exercise equally with men. Concomitantly with this movement, however,—and beginning indeed, very much earlier, and altogether apart from any conscious "movement" at all,—there was a tendency to change the laws in a direction more favourable to women and their personal rights, especially as regards marriage and property. These legal reforms were effected by Parliaments of men, elected exclusively by men, and for the most part they were effected without any very strong pressure from women. It had, however, long been claimed that women themselves ought to have some part in making the laws by which they are governed, and at this stage, towards the middle of the last century, the demand for women's parliamentary suffrage began to be urgently raised. Here, however, the difficulties naturally proved very much greater than they were in the introduction of a higher level of education for women, or even in the opening up to them of hitherto monopolised occupations. In new countries, and sometimes in small old countries, these difficulties could be overcome. But in large and old countries, of stable and complex constitution, it was very far from easy to readjust the ancient machinery in accordance with the new demands. The difficulty by no means lay in any unwillingness on the part of the masculine politicians in possession; on the contrary, it is a notable fact, often overlooked, that, in England especially, there have for at least half a century been a considerable proportion of eminent statesmen as well as of the ordinary rank and file of members of Parliament who are in favour of granting the suffrage to women, a much larger proportion, probably, than would be found favourable to this claim in any other section of the community. That, indeed,—apart from the delay involved by ancient constitutional methods, —has been the main difficulty. Neither among the masculine electors nor among their womenfolk has there been any consuming desire to achieve women's suffrage.

The result has been a certain tendency in the Woman's Movement to diverge in two different directions. On the one hand, are those who, recognising that all evolution is slow, are content to await patiently the inevitable moment when the political enfranchisement of women will become possible, in the meanwhile working towards women's causes in other fields equally essential and sometimes more important. On the other hand, a small but energetic, sometimes even violent, section of the women engaged in this movement concentrated altogether on the suffrage. The germs of this divergence may be noted even thirty years back when we find Miss Cobbe declaring that woman's suffrage is "the crown and completion of all progress in woman's movements, while Mrs. Cady Stanton, perhaps more wisely, stated that it was merely a vestibule to progress. In recent years the difference has become accentuated, sometimes even into an acute opposition, between those who maintain that the one and only thing essential, and that immediately and at all costs, even at the cost of arresting and putting back the progress of women in all other directions, is the parliamentary suffrage, and on the other hand, those who hold that the suffrage, however necessary, is still only a single point, and that the woman's movement is far wider and, above all, far deeper than any mere political reform.

Introduction

It is at this stage that Ellen Key comes before us with her book on *The Woman's Movement*, first published in Swedish in 1909, and now presented to the reader in English. As Ellen Key views the Woman's Movement, it certainly includes all that those who struggle for votes for women are fighting for; she is unable to see, as she puts it, why a woman's hands need be more soiled by a ballot paper than by a cooking recipe. But she is far indeed from the well-intentioned but ignorant fanatics who fancy that the vote is the alpha and the omega of Feminism; and still less is she in sympathy with those who consider that its importance is so supreme as to justify violence and robbery, a sort of sex war on mankind generally, and the casting in the mud of all those things which it has been the gradual task of civilisation to achieve, not for men only but for women. The Woman's Movement, as Ellen Key sees it, includes the demand for the vote, but it looks upon the vote merely as a reasonable condition for attaining far wider and more fundamental ends. She is of opinion that the Woman's Movement will progress less by an increased aptitude to claim rights than by an increased power of self-development, that it is not by what they can seize, but by what they are, that women, or for the matter of that men, finally count. She regards the task of women as constructive rather than destructive; they are the architects of the future humanity, and she holds that this is a task that can only be carried out side by side with men, not because man's work and woman's work is, or should be, identical, but because each supplements and aids the other, and whatever gives greater strength and freedom to one sex equally fortifies and liberates the other sex.

Certainly we may not all agree with Ellen Key at every point, nor always accept her interpretation of the great movement of which she is so notable a pioneer. The breadth of her sympathies may sometimes seem to lead to an impracticable eclecticism, and, in the rejection of narrow and trivial aims, she may too sanguinely demand an impossible harmony of opposing ideals. But if this is an error it is surely an error on the right side. She has not put forward this book as a manifesto of the advanced guard of the Woman's Movement, but merely as the reflections of an individual woman who, for nearly half a century, has pondered, felt, studied, observed this movement in many parts of the world. But it would not be easy to find a book in which the claims of Feminism —in the largest modern sense—are more reasonably and temperately set forth.

Havelock Ellis.

LONDON, May 1, 1912.

CONTENTS

		PAGE
INTRODUCTION	. . . . . .	1

CHAPTER

I   The External Results of the Woman Movement 23

II   The Inner Results of the Woman Movement 58

III   The Influence of the Woman Question upon Single Women . . 71

IV   The Influence of the Woman Movement upon the Daughters . . 89

V   The Influence of the Woman Movement upon Men and Women in General 111

VI   The Influence of the Woman Movement upon Marriage . . . 139

VII   The Influence of the Woman Movement upon Motherhood . . 169

The Woman Movement

INTRODUCTION

THE first "woman movement" was Eve's gesture when she reached for the fruit of the Tree of Knowledge—a movement symbolic of the entire subsequent woman's movement of the world. For the will to pass beyond established bounds has constantly been the motive of her conscious as well as of her subconscious quest. Every generation has called this transgression, this passing beyond the bounds, a "fall of man," the "original sin," a crime against God's express command, a crime against the nature of woman as prescribed for her for all time.

And yet from the beginning women have appeared who have passed far beyond the established boundaries set for their sex by their era and upheld by their own people. They have demonstrated that limitations thus prescribed do not always coincide with what is considered by the majority to be the "nature" of woman. At one time a woman has manifested the "masculine" characteristics of a ruler or has performed a "masculine" deed; at another time she has distinguished herself in "masculine" learning or art, or again has dared to love without the permission of law and custom. In a word the individual woman, when her head or her heart was strong enough, has always shown the possibilities of the development of personal power. But she has had in that effort only her own strength and her own will upon which to rely; she has neither been urged on by the spirit of her time (*Zeitgeist*) nor been emulated by the masses. Exceptional women have sometimes been glorified by their contemporaries and by posterity as "wonders of nature"; sometimes been cited as "warning examples." Seen in connection with the world's woman movement all these instances, where a bond was broken by woman's power of mind or creative gift, by a heart or a conscience, are parts of what can be called the "prehistoric" woman movement. This movement for personal freedom formed no step in that phase of the development which possesses a conscious purpose, but was merely sporadic. Even so the participation was long nameless which women took in the great struggles for freedom where, without consideration for the "nature" of woman, they dared bleed upon the arena and scaffold, ascend the pyre, and be raised upon the gibbet. Very rarely did these women martyrs alter immediately men's—or even women's—conception of woman's "being." But just as many perfumes are dissipated only after centuries, so there are also deeds whose indirect results persist through centuries.

Most significant, however, upon the whole in the "prehistoric" woman movement, are innumerable women whose souls found expression only in the strong, quiet acts of every day life but yet remained living and growing. As a reason for the "enslavement" of woman by man, the primitive division of labour is still occasionally cited. This division of labour made war and the chase man's task and so developed in him courage, energy, and daring, while the woman remained the "beast of burden." But we forget that, in this labour arrangement, the handicraft and husbandry which woman practised at that time made her, to perhaps a higher degree than man, the conservitor of civilisation and probably developed her psychic power in more comprehensive manner than his.

Even after this division of labour ceased there remained—and remain still in innumerable country households—in and through many of the important and difficult tasks of the mother of the house, numerous possibilities for spiritual development. And exactly in this respect industrial work robs the woman of much.

By the side of these innumerable nameless women who, century after century, in and through the material work of culture which they performed, increased their psychic power, we must remember all the unnamed women who with flower-like quiet mien turned their souls to the light.

Antique sepulchres and Tanagra figures tell us more about the harmonious, refined corporeality of the Hellenic woman than the famous statues of Aphrodite or Athena. In like manner it is not the illustrious but the nameless women who most clearly reveal the will of the woman soul, in antiquity, for light and life.

Numbers of Greek women were disciples of the philosophers, some even were their inspiration. Generally courtesans, these women represented the "emancipation" of that time from the servile condition of the legitimate married women and also showed that women already longed to share in the interests of men and to acquire their culture. History has preserved also words and deeds of wives and mothers of the past which show that these also at times attained "masculine" greatness of soul and civic virtue. Pythias and Sibyls, Vestals and Valas, are other witnesses that the power of woman's soul was active and recognised long before Christianity. Even among the purely primitive races there were found—and are found—cases in which woman in power and rights was placed, not only on an equality with man, but even above him. And if, on the one hand, the rigid exactions which men from the earliest time have fixed upon the wife's fidelity—while they themselves had full freedom for promiscuity—show that the wife was considered as the property of the husband, so, on the other hand, this very conception was a means of elevating and refining the soul life

Introduction

of woman. For the self-control which she had to impose upon herself deepened her feeling for a devotion which embraced only one, the man to whom she belonged. Nothing would be more superficial than to estimate the real position of woman, among any special people, only by what we know of their laws. It is as if one, in a few centuries from now, should judge the actual position of the modern European wife by referring it to the wretched marriage laws which now obtain. They forget the deep gulf between law and custom who declare that marriage devotion, veneration for the sanctity of the home, esteem for the spiritual being of the wife first arose as a result of Christianity.

It is significant enough for the freeing of woman that Jesus raised the personal worth of *all* mankind through His teaching that—whoever or whatever the person in outer respects may be—every soul possesses an eternal value comprised, as it were, in God's love; significant enough that Jesus Himself, because of this point of view, treated every woman, even the sinner, with kindness and respect. Because of the increasing uncertainty concerning the real ideals of Jesus, one is compelled to assume that—just as Veronica's handkerchief preserved the imprint of Jesus' outer image—the manner of life of the oldest Christian communities has preserved the imprint of His teaching. It is significant of their doctrines that in these communities women and men stood side by side in the same faith, in the same hope, in the same exercise of love, and in the same martyrdom. Here was "neither man nor woman," but all were one in the hope of the speedy second coming of Jesus to establish God's Kingdom.

But the more this hope faded, the more the Pagan-Jewish conception of woman again made itself felt. It is true the Church sought to place man and woman on an equality in regard to certain marriage duties and rights; to uphold on both sides the sanctity of marriage; to protect women and children against despotism. It is true the Church strove to counteract crude sensuality, utilising, among other things, an emphasis of celibacy as the expression of the highest spirituality.

But, on the other hand, the doctrine of this Church became the greatest obstacle to the elevation of woman, because it lessened the reverence for her mission as a being of sex. Marriage, the only recognised ends of which were the prevention of unchastity and the propagation of the race, was looked upon as an inferior condition in comparison with pure virginity. And the more this ideal of chastity was extolled, the more woman was degraded and considered the most grievous temptation of man in his striving after higher sanctity. Before God, so man taught, man and woman were truly equal; but not in human relationships or qualities; yes, and man has gone in this direction even to the point of debating the question in church councils, as to whether woman really had a soul or not!

Introduction

But when the Church revered pure virginity in the person of the Mother of Jesus, it was woman in highest form—as happy or suffering mother—that the Church unconsciously glorified. In the statues and altar pieces of the cathedral man worships, in the likeness of Mary, the purest and noblest womanhood. The virtues especially extolled by the Church were also those in which Mary in particular and woman in general had pre-eminence. By all these impressions a soul condition was created in which the heart penetrated by religious ecstasy, must, of psychological necessity, devote itself to the earthly manifestations of this same pure womanhood. Generally this devotion was only an ecstatic cult, an adoration from afar of an ideal, inspiring deeds or poetry. Sometimes this ecstasy fused the being of man and woman in the sensuous-soulful unity of great love. But when neither was the case, yet the adoration of knights and minnesingers increased the esteem of man for woman and the esteem of woman for herself. It also contributed to the esteem of man for woman that, as the men were always obliged to stand in arms, they could rarely acquire the learning which the priests—and through them the wives and daughters of the castles—acquired. The superiority of woman in this respect had a refining influence upon manners and customs and upon the general culture of the time. Often through a number of women auditors the poem of a minnesinger first became famous. When in Mainz one sees Heinrich Frauenlob's tombstone, one comprehends, through the soulful noble lines, how mourning women bore him to the grave, as the little bas-relief at the base of the stone represents. Their sympathy made him their singer and his sympathy revealed, to their time and to themselves, their own being. Woman's ideal of love became through poetry and courts of love the ideal also of the most cultured men. We see here a movement of the time which women already half consciously effected by their life of feeling and their culture. The authority which the wife exercised as lady of the manor during the absence, often of many years' duration, of her husband gave her increased power to disseminate about her that finer culture which she herself had gained. But when the lords of the manor returned and again assumed power, then indeed at times strange thoughts might have come to their wives, while they fixed their glance, under the great arched eyelids, upon the missal or the romance of chivalry or, with long tapering fingers, moved the chessmen or played the harp, or while they bent the slender white neck over the embroidery frame or the lace-pillow upon which they wrought veritable marvels of handicraft. Perhaps even then there stirred under many a brow the presentiment of a time in which the relationship between man and woman would be different. Such thoughts must have arisen also in the manor-houses when the men began to arrogate to themselves one handicraft after

Introduction

another, occupations which in earlier times the daughters once learned from their fathers, at whose side they sometimes even entered the guild. Could even the nun's veil prevent such thoughts from rising between the white temples of some of the women who—suffering or superfluous outside in the world—had found refuge in the cloister? Here was accomplished most peacefully the "emancipation," of that time, of the intellectual and artistic gifts of woman, for whom religion and the life of the cloister had always employment. And if the soul of a nun was greater and richer than usual, then might it indeed have happened that she devoted herself to meditation, in a quandary as to whether all of God's purposes for the gifts of her soul were truly fulfilled. And this the more intently since even then many women outside the cloister—women whose religious inspiration directed their genius to great ends—outside in the world, exercised a powerful influence upon the thought as upon the events of their time and, after death as saints, retained power over souls. Our Birgitta, for example, possessed herself of a great part of "woman's rights."

So significant had the psychic power of woman shown itself to be in the Middle Ages that already in the early Renaissance it brought forth a number of "feminist" writers, both women and men. And in the height of the Renaissance there was quite an "emancipation" literature, about women and by women. This literature increased during the following centuries. Famous men emphasised the importance of a higher education of woman; some, as early as the beginning of the 16th century, claimed the absolute superiority of woman in all things. Greater freedom, education, and rights, in one or another respect, were demanded by men as well as women "feminists." This literature purposed less, however, to alter some given conditions than, by means of examples of famous women of antiquity, to demonstrate the personal right and the social gain of what already obtained without hindrance, although with the disapproval of many:—that numbers of women had appeared who in classic culture, in the practice of learned professions, in political or religious, intellectual or æsthetic interests, stood beside the men of Humanism, the Renaissance, and the Reformation.

The ideal of the time, the fully developed human personality of marked individuality, determined the conduct of life of women exactly as that of men. Both sexes cherished the life-value which the original, isolated, individual personality signified for other such personalities. Both sexes appropriated to themselves the right to choose that which was harmonious with their own natures, that which soul or sense, thought or feeling, desired. It followed from this conception that women sought to attain the highest degree of the beauty and grace of their own sex and at the same time to cultivate what "manly" courage or genius nature had given them—attributes which men valued in them next to their purely womanly qualities.

But at this time it was not the *work* of woman which had the great cultural significance, but the human essence of her being reflected in *the works of men.* In antiquity woman exhibited the manly qualities of greatness of soul and civic virtue; in the Middle Ages she revealed the same faculty as man for saintliness and exercise of love; in the Renaissance she manifested the same ability as man to mould her own personality into a living work of art. If the spirit of equality between the sexes, which prevailed in the Renaissance, had further directed the progress of development, a "woman movement" would never have arisen, because its ends, which are to-day still contended for, would have been attained one after another, at the appointed time, as natural fruits of the florescence of the Renaissance.

As it is, this florescence acquired only very slight *immediate* influence upon the emancipation of woman—and the farther North one goes the slighter it becomes. The periods of the Counter-Reformation, of the Religious Wars and of the new Orthodoxy, on the contrary, had as result an enormous retrogression in the position of woman.

The "Deliverance of the Flesh," which was accomplished by the verdict of Protestantism upon the life of the cloister, and by its support of marriage, had little in common with the deep feeling for the right and beauty of corporeality by which the Renaissance, intoxicated with life, became the era of the great renascence of art. Luther's conception of the sex life, as "sanctified" by marriage, was so crassly utilitarian that it again dragged woman down from that high level upon which the finest life of feeling and culture of the Middle Ages and of the Renaissance had placed her.

As matron of the household, woman retained her authority. The rational, common-sense marriage was the one most conformable to this literal doctrine of Luther, and the most usual. To the man who had chosen her, the wife bore children by the dozen and threescore. The Church gave her soul nourishment. If a woman occasionally sought to exercise her spiritual gifts in a "worldly" direction, she needed powerful protection, else she ran the danger of being burned as a witch!

Yet in spite of all, even this period produced not a few women who procured for themselves the learning after which they thirsted, who succeeded in keeping their souls alive, in finding springs in the midst of the stony wastes of the desert. The more, however, the different branches of learning developed, and especially as Latin became the language of the learned, the more difficult it became for women to force their way to these springs, sealed for the majority of their sex. For a classical education became more and more infrequently extended to the daughter, for whom even the ability to read and write was considered a temptation to deviation from the path of virtue.[1]

That women in time of persecution adhered to the new doctrine with warm belief and suffered for it with the whole strength of their souls, that in time of war they managed house and estate with power and understanding, altered in no respect, at the time, woman's social or marriage position. Man was woman's sovereign master and therefore a good bit nearer God than she. In marriage woman was considered, according to the bishop's word, "man's chattel," outside of marriage as a tool of the devil. But however deeply the soul of woman was oppressed at this time, yet it still lived and endowed sons, in whom the strong but unexercised endowments of the mother became genius; it endowed daughters, who secretly procured sustenance for their souls and who in turn transmitted their rebellious spirit to a daughter or granddaughter.

When at the end of the period of Orthodoxy and Absolutism, the great fundamental principle of Protestantism, the principle of personality, once more made headway, one of the most characteristic expressions of this reaction is that, in England, Milton wrote upon the right of divorce and Defoe

[1] In the summer of 1909 I sat in a Swedish home where the grandmother, for this reason, had never learned to write but where the granddaughter read aloud the thesis for her bachelor's examination. One hears even to-day of customs and points of view in certain farms and manses which faithfully imitate those of the time of the Reformation.

upon the right of woman to the development and exercise of her mental powers. Among others who demanded greater education for women were Comenius in Germany and Fénelon in France. It was not in the former country that woman, so long oppressed, first won her great cultural influence. That happened in the land where women had never wholly lost it. In France, in the age of enlightenment, it was the salons created by women that determined the European spirit of the time. Letters and memoirs indicate sufficiently the influence of woman—in good as well as in bad sense—in politics and literature, manners, customs, and taste. Women transform indirectly the political, philosophic, and scientific style. For they demand that every subject be treated in a manner easily comprehensible and agreeable to them. A number of writings appeared which aimed to make it easy for "women folk" also "to be freed through the reason."

Since it was the approval of women which determined fame, men were only too eager to fulfil their expressed demands. Women disseminated the ideas of men in wide circles, partly by buying their writings in great numbers and distributing them, partly also by social life. Never has woman more perfectly accomplished the important task of adjusting culture values. The art of conversation, developed to the highest perfection, was, it is true, often only a game of battledore and shuttlecock with ideas. But it performed at the same time, and in more elegant and more effective manner, a great part of the office of to-day's Press. The political leader, art and literary criticism, gossip (*causerie*), the "portrait gallery" of contemporaries—all this was gathered from clever discourse. Through their art of conversation the women became—next to the philosophers and statesmen who in this or that salon were the leading spirits—the intellectual leaders of the time; they created "enlightened opinion," they co-operated finally in the Revolution. The mistresses of these salons scarcely felt the need of an emancipation of woman; for they had for themselves as many possibilities of culture, of development of their powers, of the exercise of their faculties, as even they themselves could wish. The intellectual curiosity, which coveted learning, and the cultural interest of these women penetrated in wider circles, and a result of this general awakening was the Woman's Lyceum founded in Paris in 1786, among the students of which were found, some years later, enthusiastic supporters of the Revolution.

Also among the German peoples there appeared, in the age of enlightenment, women with literary and scientific interest; some with extraordinary gifts which they also exercised. But for the most part women and men under more clumsy social forms, so called "Academies" and "Societies," engaged in their "learned pastime"; and nowhere, except in the person of some ruler, did woman attain in Europe, in the age of enlightenment, an influence which can be compared to that of the French women.

In the midst of the period of rococo elegance and gallantry, of reason and esprit, came the great regeneration, the second Renaissance—the Revival of Feeling. This occurred first in the field of religion, through the pietistic movement of the time. Later it was Rousseau who, in connection with religion, nature, love, motherhood, became the liberator of feeling, and together with him were the English "sentimental" poets and the German poetry, which reached its culminating point in Goethe. Literature, the Theatre, and Art came more and more to the front and, by that means, women acquired greater possibilities of becoming acquainted with, understanding, and loving the richest culture of the time.

And with this Revival of Feeling, personal freedom, individual character, became again the great life value. Women who wish to give expression to their feeling in their life now become more numerous: women who are conscious that their being buries many unsatisfied demands, not only in connection with the right of culture of their natural character, but also in connection with the right, in private life and in society, to give expression to this natural character. Men are continually in intellectual interchange with women, giving as well as receiving; woman nature is esteemed with ever finer comprehension.

Since feelings determine thoughts—for the

Introduction

thought always goes in the direction in which the feeling says happiness is to be found—so it is natural that, in the second half of the 18th century, the idea of freedom is the ideal which kindles the soul of increasing numbers of women. *The emancipation of the individual* is the tale within the tale, from the Renaissance up to the struggles of the Reformation for freedom of conscience, freedom of learning, freedom of investigation, and freedom of thought. Then finally came the struggle for constitutionally protected civic freedom. In America as early as 1776 the demand for the enfranchisement of women was raised, because they had taken part in the struggle for freedom with such great enthusiasm and constancy. With the same passion they threw themselves into the struggle in France for the "Rights of Man." But both times they had to learn to their sorrow that "fellow-citizen" and "man" were terms which as yet referred only to men. That a woman during the French Revolution proclaimed "Women's Rights," that women discussed these questions as well as questions of education and other vital questions, with ardour, had as little immediate effect as the attempt at that time to enforce the right of the fourth estate. These sorely oppressed movements, of women and of working men, dominate the 19th century and now at the beginning of the 20th have every reason for assurance of victory.

In the 17th and 18th centuries men and women

writers appeared in different countries to demonstrate and establish the worth and right of woman as "man." Indirectly inspired by the great women of the earlier centuries, they were immediately influenced by woman's political and cultural exercise of power in the 18th century. Especially notable are the arguments which were advanced in the 90's of the 18th century by writers manifestly uninfluenced by one another—the Swede, Thorild, in *The Natural Nobility of Womankind;* the German, Hippel; the Frenchman, Condorcet; the English woman, Mary Wollstonecraft. All insist that difference in sex can form no obstacle to placing woman on an equality with man in the family and in society; that she shall have the same right as man to education and free agency. The men writers emphasised more her individual human right, as "man," and the advantage to society; the women writers more the mother's need of culture and her right to it, in order to be able to rear and protect her children better. But all four ideas are, at heart, determined by the same point of view which the great philosopher of evolution thus formulated later: *the fundamental condition for social equilibrium is the same as for human happiness and lies in the law of equal freedom.* And this means that every one—without regard to difference between sex and sex, man and man—must have the right and the opportunity to develop and exercise his own capacities. For no one to-day can undertake so certain a valuation of talents that this valuation could justify society in restricting, a priori, the right of a single one of its members *to develop* his capacities, even though these capacities might take such a direction, later, that society would be compelled to limit their *exercise*.

Spencer arrived by the deductive method at the same demand Romanticism reached earlier by the intuitive method. Romanticism recognised that in the measure in which the individual is unusual he must be also unintelligible, for he shows to the majority only his surface; his innermost soul only to those in harmony with him. Even in the family circle the individual often remains therefore undiscovered. How much more then must society, composed for the most part of Philistines, outrage the individual if it concedes rights to one category, to one sex, to one class, and not to the other!

And from this point of view the Romanticists drew for women also the logical conclusion of individualism. They pointed out that the sex character, carried *to the extreme*, furnished neither the highest masculine nor the highest feminine type; that each sex must develop in itself both noble human *universality* and individual *peculiarity*. And this the great woman personalities did who shared the destiny of the Romanticists. They were thereby fully and wholly able to share also the intellectual life of their husbands. Love became thus a unity of souls. The romantic ideal of love was expressed in *La Nouvelle Héloise*, in Goethe's letters to Charlotte von Stein, in Rahel, in Mme. de Staël. It was found in the first half of the 19th century in many great women; for example, George Sand, Elizabeth Barrett Browning, Camilla Collett. It appeared in Shelley and in the Swedish poet Almquist, in Stuart Mill and Robert Browning, also in certain French and German poets and thinkers. This ideal has now been for some centuries the ideal of most women and of not a few men of feeling.

But since a truly psychic unity is possible only between two beings who are, in outer as in inner sense, *free*, exactly for this reason, "romantic love" has as consequence the demand for the emancipation of woman.

The love of Romanticism, which has been caricatured to the extent that it signified only moonshine, ecstasy, sonnets, and wife barter, had its real essence in the desire for completeness of soul in love. This was, in a new form, the ideal of the courts of love. But since completeness of soul means that all the powers of the soul can freely and fully penetrate and elevate one another, so the first requisite for that soulful love was that *woman's* thinking as well as her feeling, her imagination as well as her will, her desire for power, as well as her conscience, be freed from the shackles imposed upon them from without, in order to be strengthened and purified. The second stipulation was that *man's* inner, spiritual life be freed from the deteriorating results of the prerogatives and prejudices accorded to and maintained by his sex.

Introduction

A new ideal in the relationship between husband and wife, between mother and child; the demand of the feminine individuality for the right to free cultivation of her powers and to self-direction; the need of new fields for this exercise of her power after industrialism began to usurp one branch of domestic work after another—these are the fundamental reasons for what is called the middle-class woman movement. The middle-class woman— because of the increasing surplus of women, because of the continually greater variety of economic conditions and the decrease in marriage for this and other reasons—was to an ever greater extent constrained to self-maintenance. Thus the *economic* reason for the woman movement, not only in the labouring class but also in the middle class, became the most effective influence operating in the *widest* circles, although the reasons mentioned previously were the first and deepest causes.

And herewith we stand at the beginning of the woman movement, become *conscious of its purpose*.

But this movement would be a stream without sources if the "anonymous" movements indicated here with the greatest brevity had not preceded, if in the grey morning of time the endless procession had not begun in which women now nameless for us walked at the head, each with an amphora upon her shoulder—amphoræ which they filled at any fountain of life. Before these nameless women vanished on the horizon, each, like a water nymph of antiquity, lowered the brim of her urn to the earth, which thus was traversed by innumerable interlacing rills. And all these—even if by the most circuitous route—have augmented by some drops the mighty stream now called the woman movement.

CHAPTER I

THE EXTERNAL RESULTS OF THE WOMAN MOVEMENT

THE history of the woman movement, conscious of its purpose, does not fall within the compass of this book. But as foundation for later judgments, it is necessary to take a short retrospective glance over the essential results which the woman movement has attained in the struggle for woman's equality with man in the right to general culture, professional education, and work, as well as in the sphere of family and of civil status. These several demands for equality were voiced, as early as 1848, in a powerful and man-indicting plea by the American women in their "Declaration of Sentiments." But in 1905 the program for Germany's "Allgemein Frauenverein," as well as many both conservative and radical resolutions for women congresses in different countries, show how far removed Europe and, in many respects, America also, still are from the desires expressed in the year 1848.

If the humble utterance of women, "We can with justice demand nothing of life except a work and a duty," be conclusive, then life has already conceded to the demands of woman in rich measure. The woman movement and the self-interest of the employers have made accessible to her a number of new fields of labour, without mentioning those which fifty years ago were the only ones "proper" for women of the middle class—those of teacher, lady companion, and "lady's help." The woman movement and man's increasing recognition of woman's need of general education and professional qualification have created a large number of educational institutions. But in regard to the right of work, the acquisitions are but insignificant if this right be defined as *the opportunity for that work which one prefers and for which one is best fitted*. Women have now, for example, in many countries the right to pass the same examinations as men, but in many cases not the right to the offices which these examinations open to men. The profession to which women have found a comparatively easy entrance, that of physician, is widely extended among women in Europe as well as in America. That a dwelling was denied to the first woman physician because her profession was considered "improper" for a woman, sounds now like a fable. Everywhere now are women nurses, teachers of gymnastics, dentists, apothecaries, and midwives. In America there are even many women ministers and it sounds likewise wholly fabulous to say that the first of these was literally stoned. Women judges also have been appointed in America. In Europe there are none to my knowledge and no women preachers. And yet the woman pastor would often be, especially for women and children, a better minister than the clergyman; for them also the woman judge might often surpass the man in penetration and understanding. The profession of law, open to women in many countries, is as yet little practised by them in Europe. And yet as advocate, police officer, and prison attendant, the female official would be of special service for her own sex as well as for children and young people of both sexes. But in every field where the living reality of flesh and blood has to be compressed into legal paragraphs, mankind must be more or less mistreated. And since even masculine jurists of feeling suffer under this conviction, the reason for the fact that this career, in which woman could be of infinitely great service to humanity, has thus far attracted her little, may be sought in feminine sensitiveness.

All the more numerous are the women who have devoted themselves to the task most akin to motherhood, the profession of teacher. Unfortunately not always the inner call but the prestige of the position has determined the choice. Millions of women are now employed as teachers in all possible types of schools, from kindergartens to training schools, from infant schools to boys' colleges. Even in universities, although in Europe very rarely it is true, women occupy chairs of learning. In the field of popular education, women are zealously active as lecturers, librarians, leaders of evening classes, and in similar work.

With every decade, woman's powers have attained their right more fully and in fields where it now seems incredible that men could, and still partly do, insist upon getting along without them. I refer to the associations and institutions connected with prison supervision and reformatories; with schools and children's homes; care of the poor and the sick; health and factory inspection. Slowly but surely the woman movement has prepared a place here for the mother of society beside the father of society who in these domains is often very awkward or quite helpless. Alone, or together with men, women have organised milk distribution and crèches, housekeeping schools, school food-kitchens, people's food-kitchens, people's polyclinics, sanitariums and rest-homes, vacation colonies, homes for sick and neglected children, etc. Many kinds of homes for working women, old people's homes, rescue homes, institutions for the protection of mothers and children, employment bureaus, legal redress, and other forms of social relief are connected, indirectly if not directly, with the woman movement. Great women agitators on their part set thousands of women into action, as for example, Harriet Beecher Stowe, agitating against negro slavery, Josephine Butler against prostitution, Frances Willard against intemperance, and Bertha von Suttner against war.

And yet in spite of the fabulous amount of time, strength, and money which the associations and organisations thus created have cost in donations of time and money, this social relief work is only the oil and wine of the Samaritan for the wounds of society. As long as brigand hands drag mothers and children into factories; as long as armies cost much more than schools; as long as dwelling conditions in the cities are for many people worse than those for domestic animals in the country; as long as alcohol and syphilis brand the new generation—so long woman's devotion remains powerless.

And this conviction has urged women to transform their social work from an often injudicious "Christian" compassion into an organised charity in order to anticipate and prevent need and to facilitate self-help. But also in this new phase of their philanthropic work many women of the middle class are arriving at an understanding of the necessity of a social reform in accordance with socialistic demands. A larger number of women join the suffragist movement, less owing to individual demands for rights than out of despair over the hopeless social work to which their feeling of solidarity still impels them. For without suffrage (this they experience every day) their work of relief is like seed sown in a morass.

A by-product of the social relief work is that many single women have found, in voluntary social work, an occupation and often also, in remunerative social work, a livelihood; in both cases through service in which certain feminine qualities can be of value.

Yes, exactly in the above mentioned fields of

work, which so often bring the modern woman in contact with the finest and most delicate as well as with the coarsest and hardest sides of life; which place her before conflicts of the most exceptional as well as of the most universally human kind— there woman has nothing *new* to give except her motherliness. That means protecting tenderness, gentle patience, glad readiness to help, the interest embracing each one in particular, the fine and quick vibration in contact with the feelings of others which we, in a word, call "tact." If, however, a woman has not been endowed with motherliness, or has none remaining, then she reverts to impersonal devotion to duty, hard formalism, dry routine; then all the talk about the *social* significance of woman's entrance into the field of medicine or jurisprudence or the ministry or social work remains only empty phrases. In all these spheres a good man is much more valuable than a hard woman. And that woman's hands can be rough, woman's eyes cold, woman's soul base or cruel— this many suffering and crushed, sorrowing and sinful, small and defenceless have already experienced. If woman is to keep her superiority as the alleviator of the suffering of others, the protector of others, solicitous for the welfare of others, then she must not only acquire certain universal human qualities in which man is often superior to her; she must also carefully guard and cultivate the best capacities which her sex gained in and through the hundred thousand years' activity as

The External Results 29

that half of mankind which created the home and reared the children.

Although the woman movement has multiplied and extended the social relief work of woman in innumerable directions, still it has not yet opened to her the field in which formerly deaconesses, and much earlier still nuns, were engaged. But what is new as result of the woman movement is that more and more single *cultured* women now devote themselves to the occupations of governess, nurse, midwife, and kindred callings; as well as that more special training is demanded for these vocations to which women turned earlier with downright criminal carelessness.

. . . . . .

Simultaneously with the need of the middle-class woman for new fields of work, came the extraordinarily rapid development of commerce and business, which occasioned the need of new working forces. Feminine honesty, orderliness, and devotion to duty—alas, also her modest demands of compensation—made the state as well as private employers favourably disposed to employ women in increasingly greater numbers in the different branches of commerce: in the post-office, railroads, telegraph, telephone, as also in banks, counting houses, agencies or stores, as secretaries, stenographers, and clerks. In cases where the wife or daughter was the husband's or father's assistant such work then received a personal interest, and what woman's labour in this form can signify for national wealth can be seen in France especially. But as a rule no real joy in work could illuminate the days and years of the generation of women who in all these vocations have grown gray and at best have been pensioned. Nevertheless, in these offices one always sees fresh faces bending over the desk to fade away in their turn.

Lack of courage or means often deters the European woman from more independent business activity, and this in spite of increasing freedom to choose her occupation, in spite of brilliant examples of successful undertakings of women, in photography, hotel or boarding-house management, dress-making, etc. In America, on the contrary, there is no masculine occupation, from that of butcher and executioner to real estate speculator and stock-exchange gambler that women have not practised.

But while the women of the older generation were thankful if only they succeeded in obtaining "a work and a duty," however monotonous and wearing it might be, the will of the younger generation for a *pleasurable* labour has fortunately increased. Partly alone, partly co-operatively, women began to venture into the applied arts, handwork, farming, or kindred work. And since corresponding special training schools quickly arise to meet the awakening of the desire for a vocation, we can hope for good results for these, as yet rare, enterprising spirits. For special education is, in our time, the essential condition of success, especially in agriculture, where the women often succeeded without other help than their personal efficiency and the "farmer's customary practice."

Since I know America only at second hand I have no claim to a final judgment regarding the influence of business life and modern methods of production upon the soul life of woman. In the women who have succeeded in securing affluence through commercial life one finds probably the same antichristian effects of this life as among men. Recently in America a number of men and women endeavoured to live for fourteen days, as Christ would have lived. The decision of most of those who were engaged in business life was that either they must cease to follow in the footsteps of Christ—or must resign their positions. And since, with due consideration for the number of woman employers in America, many of these experiences must surely have been made under feminine supervision, the exp riment does not lack a certain significance for the forming of a judgment in the direction referred to.

The zeal of women's rights advocates to open to women all of man's fields of labour, and not only this but to prove that these fields are *as well adapted* to woman as man—this zeal has unfortunately had as result that the woman movement has turned the aptitude of many women in a wrong direction and has fettered a great amount of woman's misused working power to thankless or galling tasks. But, on the other hand, how the woman movement has elevated woman's work, since it has raised the standard of qualification in many fields and increased the feeling of responsibility in all! How it has increased the honour of work and the capacity for organisation, developed the judgment, stimulated the will power, strengthened the courage! It has awakened innumerable slumbering talents, given freedom of action to innumerable shackled powers. And thus it has transformed hosts of women of the upper class, formerly the most useless burden of earth, into productive members of society, instead of mere consumers; made them self-supporting instead of dependent, joyful instead of weary of life.

. . . .

The woman movement of the lower classes is socialistic. It has increased in extent and significance in the same measure in which the working woman has given up farming, housework, and domestic service for industry.

This woman movement also worked in two directions. The older program reads: "Full equality of woman with man." In the "state of the future" both sexes shall have the same duty of work and the same protection of work, while the children are reared in state institutions.

The movement in the other direction purposes to win back the wife to the husband, the mother to the children, and, thereby, the home to all.

The old or right wing of the middle-class woman movement, as well as the older direction of socialism just mentioned, still uphold, with arguments of the old liberalism, the "individual freedom" of the working woman against all protecting "exceptional laws." Increasing numbers of the more radical—that means in this connection more social—feminists of the upper class, however, stand side by side with the less dogmatic trend of socialism in its supreme struggle for the protection of the mother.

In the socialistic woman movement, both efforts for freedom were interwoven—that of the working men and that of women—checked during the French Revolution but soon after revived as the two great forces of the new century. In this intertwining of the woman question with the labour question is found the explanation of the fact that socialists characterise the woman question as an *economic* question solely; while in reality the woman question, *historically*, manifestly began as an advocacy of the human right and worth of woman; and that too before any great industry appeared on the horizon. As long as the man was the one who, outside the home, was producer and provider, and the woman the one who, within the home, managed and perfected the raw material, no *economic* woman question could arise, but on the other hand exactly a question of *woman's rights*. For, as some writers demonstrated, as early as the 18th century it was absurd, if woman's work in the home was so valuable and so faithfully performed, that it should not secure in consequence corresponding rights. And exactly because the middle-class woman movement tried to uphold and defend the right and the freedom of women in the compass of the old society, this movement became, and must still often be, a struggle of women against men. The socialistic woman movement is on the other hand merely a factor in a *joint struggle of men and women against the old society and for a new condition*. The struggle here cannot be sex against sex, but class against class. Each of these woman movements has been partly right, each has partly misunderstood the other. Only in recent times has a convergence between the middle class and the socialistic woman movements been accomplished for the attainment of a number of common ends; for example, the protection of the mother, mentioned above, and especially the franchise. This convergence has dissolved the prejudice on both sides. In both quarters they begin to understand the power and aim of the other movement.

Socialism and the woman movement are two mighty streams which drag along with them great parts of the firm formations which they touch. But if one wishes to be just toward both, one must not forget that in this way new lands are created.

The socialistic women on their part, as speakers, agitators, journalists, members of special associations, have stood in rank and file beside the men as true comrades, and the middle-class women have much to learn from the feeling of solidarity of the women socialists. The masculine comrades have not always *in practice* substantiated the principle of equality, for even the socialist is first man and then comrade; but *in theory* he has generally supported it.

Through socialism, feminism has penetrated to the masses. What the middle-class woman movement would have needed another century to effect, socialism has accomplished in a few decades. Nothing shows better than its fear of socialists how blindly prejudiced was the right wing of middle-class feminism. And nothing so clearly elucidates in what stage of feminism the upper-class movement was than its obstinate adherence to "the principle of personal freedom" in face of the atrocious actual conditions which resulted from the "freedom of work" of the women factory hands.

I will here recall only in brief the progress of the economic woman movement in the class of factory workers. When machines transformed the whole method of production and a host of women no longer found sufficient occupation in the home, while at the same time the possibilities of marriage decreased because of the surplus of women and also for other reasons, the middle-class women looked about them for new fields of labour. The great industries in return looked about them for more "hands." And since, with the machine, female hands were quite as serviceable as male—with a new machine it was possible to replace thirty men with one woman—and since in addition they were cheaper, then began that exodus of women from the home into the factory, the results of which we are now experiencing.

When the mother is absent from the home, then there is lacking the cohering, supervising, warming force, and the home deteriorates and falls to pieces; the children are neglected, the husband suffers; the street takes possession of the children, the alehouse of the men. Moreover, the women work often for starvation wages, whereby less comes into the home than is lost by the absence and incapacity of the mother. In the middle classes daughters and wives, entirely or partly supported in the home, could be satisfied with smaller wages and have thus become the competitors of men and women wholly self-supporting. For the same reason wives working in these industries have often become the competitors of men, children again the competitors of women, and married women the competitors of unmarried.

In woman, so long secluded in the sphere of the family, the social feeling of solidarity has been very slowly awakened. Therefore, organisation which could prevent the competition just mentioned has only in the last decade made great progress everywhere among working women. In the middle-class vocations this is almost entirely lacking. Among the working women slowness of

The External Results

organisation is natural, for the more wretched their position was, the more difficult was it for them to organise. But among middle class women the reason was partly their individualism, partly their anti-socialism, partly the lack of feeling of solidarity just referred to.

Home work for profit and pleasure in one's own family or in service of the applied arts has become a means for the "sweat system," the facts of which belong to the darkest side of modern working life. These facts alone would be sufficient to prove that *working women* have little to gain from the luxury of the rich, an assertion with which luxury often vindicates itself. There is still for the women working at home as well as for the women working in the factory, beside their professional work, also the duty of caring for the children and managing the home. However insufficient this may be yet it still claims a great part of their already meagre leisure; and the more tender and conscientious the mothers are, the more they wear themselves out, and the sooner must society, after night-watching, lack of light and hunger have ruined them, maintain them as infirm or paupers. The life of these women passed in the factory often from childhood has made them moreover, generation after generation, more unfitted for household work. What does it profit to attempt to remedy the evil by housekeeping schools and instruction in the care of children? For where time and strength are lacking the home has lost its right.

What can be expected of women who three or four days after confinement must again stand at the machine, who are compelled to leave their children behind them, shut in at home, exposed to all conceivable accidents? What can be expected of mothers, who have become mothers against their will,—mothers of children, who because of the conditions of their parents' work have become scrofulous, rickety, idiotic—children who contract degeneration of the liver because the harassed, ignorant mother quieted them with brandy, ill-treated them,—herself a physical and psychic ruin who spreads destruction about her!

The feminists are accustomed to rage over the custom which formerly condemned the Indian widows to be burned upon the funeral pyre—a custom which is only an innocent sport in comparison with the woman slavery which Europe has even brought to a system and which the woman movement long ignored.

To these general facts, which apply also to women employed in hard agricultural labour, there is also added an entirely new series of evils associated with occupations dangerous to health—for example those in which lead, quicksilver, phosphorus or tobacco poison the workers,[1] or those branches of work where inhaling dust at the weaving loom or in spinning, breathing gas and coal smoke, exposed to heat, smoke and damp, they

[1] Next to the textile industry, the tobacco industry employs the most women.

contract tuberculosis and other diseases; to say nothing of the physical and moral misery in which miners and stevedors live. But the worst begins only when the women are to become mothers. Either the embryo is killed by an abortion, intentional or caused by the occupation; or it comes into the world dead or sick or crippled; or it dies in the first weeks or wastes away under artificial nourishment—in England for example only one out of eight children is nursed. The mothers either cannot or will not. Next to the labour conditions, alcohol plays the greatest part in this indirect massacre of infants.

If one turns from the women engaged in industrial work to the servant class, then female drudgery reaches perhaps its height among the girls employed in bars, cafés, and similar establishments. What physical and psychic results this work entails can be divined from the fact that, in England, half of all women suicides are such waitresses under 30 years of age. That family servant girls are allowed to sleep in closets and to work far beyond the present customary factory time; that in the class of saleswomen, especially in cigar shops, the longest working hours together with the most paltry starvation wages are found—all this, as every one knows, is the fundamental reason why the path is so short from all these occupations to the lowest—to prostitution. The servant girl corrupted by the master of the house, the half-starved, overworked shop girl, the night-watching cigar worker, and many, many others are found here as sacrifices of a shameless exploitation. Herewith we stand before that "woman question" in which both elementary instincts have united for that captivity of woman from which the woman movement has found no means of emancipation; against which the means sought in these and other quarters prove fruitless. For only a radical transformation of society and sexual ethics can here provide a remedy

. . . .

Every one in face of these facts, touched upon thus superficially, must be astounded that women could oppose laws for the protection of women. Fortunately these progress-impeding emancipation women had no influence when, in England and other countries, certain night work began to be prohibited to women, their working hours limited, certain employments barred out, and a time of rest assured to the woman recently confined. Still very small steps only, but in the right direction. At the same time the organisation of working women advances so that by labour unions and strikes here and there they have succeeded in enforcing better wages, shorter working hours, and better labour conditions. And so long as the woman movement of the upper classes has no solidarity with that of the lower, the female factory inspector can accomplish very little, as a result of the fear of the working women to give facts and the adroitness of the employers in veiling these. But if women of the upper class begin to compete with the slave-driving, sweat-system employers through *well-organised co-operative enterprises*, especially for the revival of artistic handwork, whereby a profitable work is made for mothers at home under good working conditions; and if they boycott all shops where the working hours of the women exceed the due measure, while their wages are below the standard; then the woman movement would be able to hasten certain reforms in the field of industry, just as so many mistresses of girls' private schools have hastened the reform of public schools: they simply availed themselves of the improvements arising from feminine initiative.

. . . .

The married woman as family provider beside the man, often also in place of the man, but always however *subservient to the man's dominion*—this is the worst form of woman slavery our time has created. The woman movement purposes indeed to make the wife "of age," in every respect, and free from the husband's guardianship. But within the woman movement all are not yet entirely agreed that *the work of the mother outside the home in and for itself is an evil*. Attempts are indeed being made to alter the conditions which are most to blame for the deterioration of mothers and children. But a large faction in the woman movement wishes still, as was said, to cling to the *immediately* remunerative work of the mother and remedy the resulting lack of home by social institutions for care of children, housekeeping, etc.

On this side, the following arguments are heard: woman becomes free only when she can wholly support herself and can devote herself to her work unhampered by duties toward husband and children; only through the reciprocal social obligation of work and the complete individual freedom of both sexes can the present conflicts between the labour of man and woman, between individual happiness and the common weal, finally cease.

Like every canalisation or drainage of the mighty river system of the life of human feeling, this program is direct and conclusive. One may easily understand that masculine brains, dominated by a passion for logic, could devise it; but if we hear it advocated by multitudes of women, then we recognise how harassed by the fourfold burden of family provider, child bearer, child educator, and housekeeper the poor women must be who can smilingly assent to the foregoing picture of the future.

And yet there is another possible ideal of the future which can be realised as soon as production is determined, no longer by private capitalistic interests, but by social-political interests. Women will then be employed in industrial fields of work where their powers are *as productive as possible* with the least possible loss in time and strength;

The External Results 43

above all in those fields where the work requires no *long* preparation and the dexterity does not suffer by *interruptions*. Before the years in which the *occupation is motherhood*, and after these years, woman can still be always remunerated by an economic wage; during the years on the contrary in which motherhood is the vocation, she can be remunerated *by the state*. It is only necessary that women and men *will* a new order whereby in the future we attain the following conditions:

A *Society*, in which the welfare of the new generation is the centre to which all social-political plans, at heart, are aiming.

Children born of parents whose souls and bodies are qualified and prepared for a worthy parenthood and who can thus create for their children sound and beautiful conditions of life.

Mothers won back to the husbands, the children, the homes, but under such circumstances that *as free human personalities they perform the most important work of society:* the bearing and rearing of children.

Fathers with time and leisure to share with the mothers the task of education and to share with them and the children the joys of the home life, as well as of the remainder of existence.

This ideal of the future state takes in my imagination the form of a varied Italian garden with a wide outlook upon the great sea. The other ideal of the future, on the contrary, is to me like a coal mine wherein all spiritual and social vegetation is petrified so that it now serves only as motive-power for machines.

. . . . . .

Nothing more effectively proves how rife with reactions—and for that reason how hidden—is the power of development, than to realise that the unorganized, inorganic socialistic ideal of the future, just mentioned, is the logical sequence of the woman movement if one draws the extreme conclusion from its fundamental idea—the right of woman to individual, free development of her powers. It is consistent historically that in America, where the movement for the right and freedom of woman has been most widely successful, many middle-class women have resolutely drawn these extreme conclusions of emancipation. Quite as psychologically logical is it, that at a time when the uncomplicated soul life and life demands of the masses still form the most important factors in the shaping of the ideal of the future, the socialistic women, from their different point of view, have arrived at like ideals. But fortunately there are in women, as in the masses, still great tracts of "new ground" where new soul conditions will germinate, and in due time, new ideals will flower. Groups of men can at times forget mankind in dwelling upon themselves. But mankind in its entirety has never yet lost the instinct for the conditions of self-preservation and the higher development of the race. I will come back later to the

The External Results

psychological phase of the question. I touch upon it here only as the social program of the future.

. . . . . .

A new field which the woman movement has opened up to woman is the scientific field. For the fact that as early as the Renaissance some Italian women occupied chairs of academic instruction, that in the 17th and 18th centuries some women devoted themselves seriously to classic studies or the exact sciences—all that was only exceptional. And the women who since the beginning of the woman movement have distinguished themselves by great services in science are still exceptional. But in many places, sometimes as assistants of their husbands or of other men, women now perform good scientific work in different lines. Many women are also active in the sphere of invention, without a single woman's name having been thus far connected with an *epoch-making* invention.

Especially where constructive ability is necessary, women have as yet not been eminent; they have created neither a philosophical system nor a new religion, neither a great musical work nor a monumental building, neither a classic drama nor an epic. On the other hand, the exact sciences, which would be considered a priori as little adapted to women, for example mathematics, astronomy, and physics, are exactly those in which thus far they have most distinguished themselves. This contains a warning against too precipitate conclusions about the intellectual life of woman. Not until several generations of women—with the same privileges of education as man, with the same encouragement from home and society—have exercised their faculty for discovery and their inventive and creative faculties can we really know whether the present inferiority of woman in this respect is a provision of nature or not; whether her genius was only hampered in its expression or whether, as I believe, it is ordinarily of a different kind from that of man.

In art there are several fields which the woman movement did not need to open for the first time to woman: dramatic art, music, and the dance. Indirectly, however, the woman movement has transformed the position of women occupied in these lines by increasing the respect for all good work of woman and raising the requirements for woman's education in general. The woman movement has also exercised an immediate influence upon certain artists of the present time. Thus Eleanora Duse said to me that her most cherished desire has been to represent and interpret the new types of women, although the dramatists of to-day have rarely given her the material she desired wherewith to create characters by which she could reveal the soul of the new woman and elevate man's, as well as woman's own, ideal of woman.

In the dance, women have been, especially in

The External Results 47

America, creative in connection with its forms and have been thereby also revelations of the new spiritual life of woman which has found expression in these forms. Great women singers, through Wagner's operas and ballad-singing, have given voice to the primeval yearning of the woman soul, as that yearning now assumes form in the new woman. And in interpretations at the hands of great pianists or violinists, not one classic musical work failed to furnish similar revelations.

The very finest effects of the woman movement—mere shades of feeling which cannot be enumerated nor discussed—have reached our present time through lines, movement, rhythm, cadence, through the timbre of a voice, the gesture of a hand, the glance of an eye, the tone of a violin. And these effects have been secured without any disturbance of the receptivity by strife over the precedence of woman or of man. In other spheres, susceptibility to the effects of art creations by woman is still often dulled by this strife. In the above named fields, long before the beginning of the woman movement, conscious of its purpose, women without arguments have convinced the world of the complete equality of woman with man. And all these women, conquering through beauty in one form or another, have done more for the woman movement than it has done for them. Certainly the woman movement both directly and indirectly has had its share in opening to women musical as well as other art academies and schools of applied arts, but academies have a doubtful value and the smaller the value, the more gifted the student. The new right has thus become dangerous to the independence of real gifts and, with all possibilities of education thus opened wide, there comes a temptation for fancied talents to pass beyond their bounds. This danger, as far as the plastic arts are concerned, has found more and more its counterpoise in the schools of applied art, by which many women have been directed to the decorative professions, from house and garden architecture to fashion designing and holiday decorations.

But in the field of the applied arts, as well as of the plastic arts and of music, the facility afforded by the modern conditions of training and of public careers has instigated many women, who before had exercised their little talent only for the pleasure of the home or society circles, to exhibit and appear publicly to the detriment both of the home circles and, alas, also of art!

The works of art by women, which humanity could not lose without really becoming poorer, have been created, thus far, neither in the sphere of music nor of plastic art; they all belong to literature. And this sphere the woman movement has not opened to woman; ever since the days of Sappho and of Corinna, women have attained fame as writers.

In letters and memoirs not originally designed

for publication, next to that in the field of romance and the novel, occasionally also in the lyric, the feminine character has found thus far its fullest and finest expression. In all these fields women have produced works which have been placed by men, not it is true beside the *greatest* works of masculine genius in the same domain, yet beside eminent works of men. As intermediary of the works of others, woman has not in our time, as in the period of enlightenment or in the circle of Goethe, her greatest significance through conversations and letters but through the printing-press. The modern woman, however, as essayist and biographer, as translator and collector, is a valuable intermediary of culture. She is also unfortunately a menace to culture, not so much because of the inferior works which she produces, for these, like the similar works of men, soon sink into oblivion. The real danger lies in the fact that women in great multitudes increase the number of those journalists who lack intellectual as well as ethical culture, which should be an imperative condition in that field of work. But this profession is now, on the contrary, the one into which the amateur may most easily force an entrance without special training and without professional reputation. The result is that men and women who lack both can pull down, in their journals, the real work and essential character of serious people, without the remotest conception or the faintest comprehension of either. On the other hand these cliques of coffee-house people crown one another as kings and queens—for a day! The press-breed carries on in leaflets its flirtation as well as its vengeance. The knife which the child of nature thrusts into a rival's breast is now transformed into the pen with which the reviewer stabs a competitor's latest work. In a word women now furnish to the Press work, occasionally excellent, frequently mediocre, all too often worthless. Their womanly characteristics make it feasible more frequently for them than for men to adopt more completely the rituals of the temple service of the deity of the Press—the Public. This "womanliness" evinces itself, especially, in the ability "to grip the fleeting moment by its fluttering locks" and also to anticipate when that moment's locks are false and so the grasp prove profitless.

While hosts of women have turned to journalism, they are seldom found in the fields to which the woman movement should have directed them: in the field of sociological and psychological research. Nearly all significant works upon the normal, the abnormal, the criminal psychic life of children, young people and women have been written by men. They have unfortunately treated the feminine spiritual life in "scientific" works also, in which the author dares speak of "woman" even though he knows nothing of her except what his own happy or unhappy experiences in a mother or sister, wife or sweetheart, have taught him.

The slight title of men to their "scientific

The External Results

method" when they venture upon the terra incognita which the soul of woman still is for them, explains why they extol, as "scientific," works of women about women which are quite as superficial as those of men themselves. With a few exceptions, it is not the physiological-psychological books written by women about women which have really taught the present something new about womankind in general and the new woman in particular. No, in the form of romances, of lyrics or in voluntary confessions, woman has contributed the most valuable documents about her sex: on the one hand those which indicate the transformations which the woman movement has occasioned in woman's nature, on the other hand those which demonstrate the extent to which her fundamental nature has remained unchanged, even though this elementary material exhibits many more facets in the modern woman than in the woman of any previous time; facets resulting from the manifold contacts and frictions with life to which woman now exposes herself or is exposed.

From a literary point of view, these books of confession have seldom a value which could be compared with that of the, in outer sense, objective, classic works which talented women writers of the present have produced. Often, however, one of these confessions, in which the writer has candidly given her own history, has been of real literary value. But even when the works contain mendacities and self-extenuations, crass injustice toward men or toward other women, as revelations of the modern woman soul they are more valuable for the future than the clarified, artistically perfect works of women, mentioned above. For the truth about woman in the century of the woman is found only in the impassioned books in which the hard struggles for freedom, work, right, or fame are recited; or in those works impassioned in another way, in which the soul or the blood or both cry out their yearning, ever unappeased, in spite of freedom and work, right and fame. What we may *to-day* rightly protest against in these books is their recklessness which may *in the future* be regarded as their greatest value.

Because, up to the present time, the most exquisite as well as the most horrifying women characters in literature have been created by men, many men think that they understand women better than women do themselves. And to this extent men are right—that women attain their most sublime heights and reach their deepest degradation in and through love. But aside from that, women have a much clearer insight and, for that reason, a much more intelligent idea of one another than man has of woman. When accordingly a woman speaks not only of herself but also of another woman—sometimes also of children—we feel already that "the eternal feminine" (*das Ewig-Weibliche*) in literature can create a feminine art, in the best meaning of the word. For the present we hope, and with good reason, that art as well as science will not appear as either masculine or feminine but reveal a complete human personality. But this does not mean that this personality has fused the masculine and feminine qualities into a common humanity and thus enervated it. No, it means that, in such a being, masculine and feminine traits exist side by side and assert themselves alternately or harmoniously in all their strength. In the rank of talent, one may find feminine men and masculine women; in that of genius, never. There each one guards fully and completely the character of his own sex in addition to the finest attributes of the other sex. The distinctively masculine or distinctively feminine attributes characterising an *earlier* culture epoch are on the contrary often lacking in these greatest men and women of their time. In other words they lack exactly those attributes, hyper-masculine or hyper-feminine, by which men and women, not abreast of the times in their development, please each other and the masses, in literature as well as in life.

In the woman-literature, directly evoked by the woman movement, we can read the whole gamut of the feminine nature, from the feminine in the highest sense to the feminine in the worst sense. This literature shows how unthinkingly and defenceless certain women have plunged into the struggle, how rationally and well equipped other women have fought it out. The impartiality of this judgment can be proven by the admission that in the first-named class I have not infrequently found adherents; in the latter class, opponents.

The woman movement itself, partly in lectures and in literary activity, partly by means of office-routine and work of organisation, has become a new *field of labour* for women. Even in this field it is found that many are called but few are chosen. But when—except after defeat—was an army ever seen without baggage?

. . . .

In the field of *family right*, the woman movement has achieved, directly and indirectly, great improvements in the legal position of the *unmarried* woman. The nearest proof is my own country. This has, within a period of from seventy to eighty years, granted to the sister the same right of inheritance as to the brother; declared the unmarried woman at her majority at the same age as man, a majority which was also expanded later through the suspension of the right of guardianship on the part of the husband, existing for married women. The marriageable age of woman was postponed to 17 years. Gradually woman has been placed on an equality with man to carry on trade and industry; she has acquired the right to hold certain public offices, although many still remain closed to her. The married woman on the contrary is still always a minor; if no marriage settlement is made the husband has the right to dispose of the wife's property; he has control of their common possessions; he can restrict her freedom of work; he has authority over the children. A few small progressive steps may nevertheless be pointed out: certain reinforcements of the effectiveness of the marriage contract; the right to her wages accorded to the wife; certain reforms in regard to the division of property and divorce; some improvements in the position of children born out of wedlock. In other countries also like reforms have been accomplished, directly, through masculine initiative; indirectly, through the influence of the woman movement. But everywhere family right is still founded upon the principles of paternal right, supremacy of the husband over the wife, indissolubility of marriage or solubility under greater or less difficulties.

In regard to citizenship I draw my examples also from the land I know best. In Sweden, women have long since participated in the choice of pastor; for about fifty years they have possessed municipal franchise; later in certain cases they have attained also municipal eligibility, for example, to the school board, board of charities, and now finally to the town council. Still others could be cited. In other countries women have sometimes more sometimes less civic right; only in a few countries have they won *political* franchise; in a single one, Finland, also political eligibility.

In the sphere of family right, as well as civic right, the woman movement has then much more remaining to conquer than it has thus far won.

But I am convinced that the little girls I see down below in the garden playing "mother and child" will possess all the rights due the wife, the mother, and the citizen.

The woman movement, in its present form, has accomplished its task if it has procured for every woman the *legal* right to develop and practise her individual characteristics unhindered because of her sex. But after this emancipation of the woman as a *human being* and a citizen, there remains her emancipation as a *woman*. And here no transformation of forms of thought and feeling, of manners and customs, attainable by any legal provisions or paragraphs, avail. The present woman movement has created and still continues to create the social *conditions* for this last emancipation. But it will not approve such far extending results of its own work. It desires the same *rights* but also the same duties for all women. If a single woman uses the freedom, which the woman movement has procured for her as a member of society, to fashion her individual life according to the deepest demands of her being, then the old guard trembles before the outcome of the battle for freedom in which it fought so valiantly.

But nothing is more certain than that the feminine personality, whether her innermost desire be spiritual creative instinct, erotic happiness, maternal bliss, or universal human goodness, will acquire ever new forms of expression: forms of expression which the once liberal, now more conservative feminists and the modern socialistic feminists partly do not divine and partly—divining—deplore! For the present even the "emancipated" woman follows as a rule the paths which social custom has marked out for her sex, as well as the cultural ideas which have been, thus far, those of man. But if, in the coming thousand years, a *feminine* culture shall really supplement the masculine, then this will be exactly in the measure in which women have the courage to create and to act as most feminists now do not even dare think. Then it will be evident that *all* social movements of the present time, especially the woman movement and socialism, are only the work of the path finder for the masculine and feminine superman or, if you prefer the older expression, *complete man*.

Like other "old guards," the veterans of feminism will not surrender but will fall upon the field of battle. The little girls there below will one day celebrate their memory. For through their struggles the way became free for youth, the way which leads out to the wide sea where perhaps shipwreck awaits the one who ventures out into the darkness with her fragile skiff. But many will brave the voyage and bide their fate, strong, proud, and composed as the maiden in Schwind's *Wasserfahrt* —that splendid symbol of the woman of the future.

CHAPTER II

THE INNER RESULTS OF THE WOMAN MOVEMENT

If I now start out to consider the woman-soul as it has developed itself under the influence of all the circumstances mentioned above, perhaps many will expect a theory about the character of the feminine soul life. But, at present, when the greatest problems of psychology are in revolution and undecided, such a theory would be as scientifically impossible as aphorisms are unanswerable. Likewise, conclusions, based upon experience, concerning the psychic peculiarity of woman would be in this chaotic transition period, superficial, if they attempted to be absolute. Only *one* decided opinion about the spiritual life of woman I cannot —in consequence of my monistic-evolutionary conception of the spiritual and physical life— refrain from expressing. This opinion is that, in the one hundred thousand years at least in which woman has practised the physical maternal functions, the spiritual attributes *essential* for motherhood must have been so strongly developed by her that this development has had, and still has always, as a result a pronounced difference between the feminine and masculine soul—that is to say, everywhere where the soul, as well as the body of a woman, is adapted and desirous of motherhood—a fitness and readiness which can still be called the *normal* condition. The spiritual qualities which maternity required have become the attributes of "womanliness," the qualities which paternity required, have become the attributes of "manliness." This difference has become quite as significant for the functional fitness of both sexes for the perpetuation and development of the race, as for the wealth of life of each new generation. The obliteration or retention of this difference is therefore a vital question for mankind.

Figuratively expressed, this seems to me the process: from a common root of universal human spiritual life issue two stems which can again unite in their blossoming. The ramification has necessarily involved a division of labour in two equally important spheres. From this point of view I give, in the following, my opinion of the value of the influence of the woman movement upon the spiritual life of woman.

We all know that life expresses itself as movement, that movement brings with it change, transformation; that this can mean quite as well disintegration as higher organisation.

The woman movement is the most significant of all movements for freedom in the world's history. The question whether this movement leads mankind in a higher or lower direction is the most serious question of the time. Those who assert unconditionally the former or the latter have uttered a premature judgment. The question must be formulated thus:

(*a*) Has the woman movement brought to mankind a higher degree of vital force, a greater faculty for self-preservation, a more complete organisation, by which the more simple forms have become more finely complex, the more uniform have become richer, more diverse; the incoherent have attained a more perfect unity? Or has the woman movement called forth an activity which represses life? degrades, scatters, and reduces the powers to uniformity, in society and in mankind?

(*b*) Is woman's spiritual life now in general above the level at which it was in the beginning of the woman movement? Have modern women finer perceptions, deeper feelings, clearer ideas, a firmer will, richer association of ideas? Do their spiritual faculties so work together that they mutually enhance instead of hinder one another? In a word is the modern woman more soulful than the woman of any other time?

(*c*) Is the body of the modern woman, at all stages of life, stronger, more healthy, and more beautiful than that of the woman of the previous century, when the woman movement began in real earnest in Europe?

(*d*) Does the modern woman perform in more perfect manner than the woman of that time, the physical and psychic functions of motherhood?

If the question be put thus then the *objective* investigator must answer to all—"*Yes and No.*"

But if this investigator is an evolutionist, then he knows that the progress of every social evolution is like that which womankind is now experiencing. We see first, how, in any given sphere of society, where those engaged therein have attained a pure, instinctive certainty in their actions through laws and customs, the individuals oppressed by these laws and customs must rebel against the limits, drawn from without, for the development and exercise of their powers. This revolt occasions at first a stage of anarchy in which everything seems to collapse—while in the previous conserving epoch "crystallisation" furnished the vital danger! But after such an anarchistic stage there comes infallibly the constructive stage, where *a part of the old is organised, incorporated, into the new.* But this acts no longer as instinctive impulse. No, mankind has become conscious anew of these values of law and custom; they have been recognised by the thought, encompassed by feeling, sanctioned by the will as still always indispensable, in another and higher form it is true than that against which the individuals rebelled. But just as the leaves which once grew green above in the summer light, gradually become one with the earth, so the motives of the new customs sink gradually down into the unknown; man acts again with instinctive certainty and uniformity—until the new period of stagnation evokes a new rebellion and achievement of individualism.

The woman movement finds itself now at a point where it is about to pass from the dynamic stage to a static stage. Exactly at this point a survey begins to be possible; and it is also necessary for every one who believes that the ideal, as well as the practical direction of the woman movement, in future, must be influenced by the knowledge gained about the effect of the movement, thus far, upon the uplifting of the life of mankind.

Every great achievement of individualism is as inconsiderate as the spring tide and must be, in order to have strength for its task. The woman movement was so also. But it encountered two other great ideas of the time, Socialism and Evolutionism, and in consequence the woman movement was obliged to modify gradually its conception of the feminine individual and of her position in existence.

On the one hand, as has been already shown, man has had to understand that "open competition" and "individual initiative" are not absolute political-economic truths. On the other hand, the defender of women's rights has been forced to understand more and more that woman's soul is no unchangeable value which must remain the same however much the spheres have changed toward which this spiritual life directed itself and from which it received its impression. While feminists fifty years ago scorned the objection that "womanliness" would be lost in business life or in politics, now the evolutionist mind in thinking women understands that all human soul life is subject to the law of change; that just as indisputably as the soul life of man is changed by different vocations and surroundings, so that of woman also must be changed. The feminists founded their dogma that the woman movement can *only benefit* woman, man, the child, the family, society, mankind upon the conviction of the *stability* of "true womanliness."

And if the woman movement had not had this religious certainty of belief, how could it have withstood the mass of prejudice and stupidity which it encountered in its own, as well as in the other sex? The woman movement has conquered because it was self-intoxicated.

And quite naturally! After a stability of centuries, during which the position of woman was altered only in and with the general progress of culture, women finally recognised that they could accelerate their own progress and with it also the somewhat snail-like course of universal human culture. And so woman asserted herself and increased her motion. The faster this movement became, the more was she seized by the intoxication which always accompanies every vigorous physical or psychic movement. And when has a movement of the time advanced more rapidly?

Folk-migrations, crusades, slave rebellions, revolutions have led a race, a class, a group, beyond certain geographical or social boundaries. The emancipation of women has shifted and extended the limits of the freedom of movement of *half mankind*. No wonder that the extent of the movement *in and for itself* was advanced as proof of the infallibility of its direction. All points of departure, the natural right of man, individual freedom, social necessity—all led out into the sun, which, in society as in nature, should radiate over woman as well as over man; they led up onto the summit where man and woman both should breathe the air of the heights. All obstacles which were raised with the help of arguments such as, "the nature of woman," "the welfare of the family," "the idea of society," "the purpose of God"—all proved temporary. And of necessity—for the innermost law of life, the law of development, of life enhancement, carried the movement forward. When it began, the Biblical expression about the wind was quoted, "Man knows not whence it comes nor whither it goes." Now all know it. Now the spirit of the time speaks with "feminist" voice. The ideas of emancipation "are in the air," like bacilli, by which only savages are thus far wholly untouched.

There are now no great movements of the time whose path does not run parallel with or cut across the woman movement. Every new generation is involuntarily and unconsciously drawn along with it. The ends already attained seem to the present age obvious; the ends, for which man is still struggling to-day, will appear equally obvious to the future. The woman movement is now a power with which even its most bitter adversaries must reckon. And this force has so quickly attained prominence exactly as a result of fanaticism. Just as the White and the Blue Nile mingle their waters in the main stream, so in every great current of time enthusiasm is mingled with fanaticism. And it is the latter which bears the most fruit, for it gives power of growth to the passions of the majority, good as well as bad.

Every great idea begins with great promulgators. The promulgator who has the spirit does not hold to the letter. And the woman movement which was spirit began also with women and men who did not follow the call of the spirit of the time; no, who from lonely heights sent out their awakening call *to* the time. Men who give their age new ideals have always religious natures. This means, according to a good definition, that they are "individualists in their being, social in their action."

Such natures burn, above all, with the passion to find themselves. Then they burn with the passion to sacrifice themselves in order to help others, whose suffering or wrongs they feel as deeply as if they were their own. No one who passively endures an injustice against himself has the material in him to struggle for the rights of others. The one who patiently forbears becomes an accessory to the injustice done to others. He who resists the injustice which he himself meets can open up the way to a higher right for others. Such path-finders were the first apostles of the emancipation of women. They consecrated to this task a faith which required no proof, a faith which saw visions and heard melodies of the glorious future that their victory would prepare for mankind. They emanated neither from scientific investigations, nor from systems of political economy, nor from philosophic evidence, nor theories of political science. They flung themselves into the struggle with inadequate weapons, without plan of campaign, just as do all impelled by the spirit. But such a method always evokes later dissension among the disciples. Sects are formed, gradually a church is crystallised, an orthodoxy, a papacy, and an inquisition. This course is physically necessary as long as mankind is still in greatest part a mass. A Paul more "Christian" than Christ and a Luther more "Paulist" than Paul are met also in the woman movement.

This has now, among most people of culture, passed beyond the stage of the great apostles and martyrs and heralds. The movement has reached the point where certain typical manifestations, certain conventional forms testify that the masses —which stoned the prophets—have now, since the ideas of the woman movement have become truisms, banalities, the fashion, appropriated them to themselves and endeavour to transform them to their image and adapt them to their needs.

Again and again the old tale repeats itself: the trolls steal the weapons of the gods but they cannot use them. Again and again there is occasion to deplore the fact that the autocrat of genius, whether he rule over a people or a kingdom of ideas, has heirs, heirs who diminish his work. Again and again it must be recognised that no spiritual formation vanishes at one blow. The servile mind, intrigue, pettiness, delusion—all that, from which the great spirits of the woman movement hoped to "emancipate" woman—could not suddenly vanish out of the world. And since all this must go somewhere it finally finds room in the woman movement itself!

But on the other side—since after all everything has another side—it must be admitted that the levelling and conserving tendency of the average person is of real value at the stage *when an idea begins to be transformed into law and custom.*

Those who can work only in crowds receive their significance *exactly because of their collective work.* They push aside the "individual emancipation" which they do not need for their own part, since they have no individuality to emancipate. But by diligent and efficient work they succeed in securing certain results, which are the common cause of all. So the Philistines make for themselves a footstool of that which was a stumbling-block for their congenial souls in the previous generation. From this height they look down upon the new truth of *their* time. And those who perceive and uphold this new truth turn aside from the great uniformed army which now advances safely where the little vanguard has previously and laboriously opened up the way. Those who turn aside will form the new vanguard when it comes to achieving, in the spirit of the first apostle, the emancipation not only of *women in the mass*, but of *each individual woman*. When the present work of the woman movement for joint, common ends shall no longer be necessary, because one end after another has been attained, then comes the task of the present "radical" feminism: the accomplishment of "emancipation" by leading it up to those free heights which already the path finders are endeavouring to attain, the heights where every feminine individuality can choose her own path of life, perhaps at variance with all others; can choose it in freedom, answerable only to her own conscience. Although this summary grouping historically as well as psychologically corresponds approximately to the past, present, and future of the woman movement, yet there are so many ramifications of the three groups into one another, that the woman movement now exhibits a tangled confusion in which every exact demarcation is impossible.

Whoever lives to witness it will see the course of progress just described—for which the modern labour movement offers quite as good material for observation as the woman movement—repeat itself in the next great emancipation movement.

I mean the movement for the right and freedom of the *child*, which will be the unconditional result of the victory of the woman and labour movements. This idea is still in the morning-clear hour of inspiration. But from the cry, "Away with the child destroying home training," we can hear that the troop of Philistines will appear by afternoon upon the scene, to adopt the idea into their midst!

By means of the comparison with socialism, I have endeavoured to emphasise that the woman movement's formation of dogmas and its doctrinary fanaticism are not effects of the peculiarity of the *feminine* mind. These phenomena are typical of every movement of the time thus far observed. They are essential above all because a new belief without dogma and without ritual is for the masses a sword without a hilt: it offers nothing tangible, nothing whereby the masses can come into relation with the idea.

That certain feminists still believe that the woman movement has advanced just as the exodus of the Children of Israel out of the land of bondage, that is to say, under God's special protection against wandering astray; that they stigmatise as "treason" and "defection" the assertion that this movement was determined by the same psychological and sociological laws as every other movement for freedom—this shows to how high a degree many leaders of the woman movement lack elementary psychological and sociological conceptions. This deficiency is, however, being continually remedied. And in the generation which now advances, dogmatic fanaticism has well nigh vanished, but pure enthusiasm is preserved.

We can thus expect from this generation a clearer understanding of the necessary *social* repressions which the woman movement has now sufficient strength to impose upon itself without forfeiting thereby its character of a *movement for freedom*. As such it cannot and dare not cease until it has attained *all* its ends. As long as the law treats women as one race, men as another, *there is a woman question*. Not until man and woman, equal and united, work together for mankind will the woman movement belong to the past.

CHAPTER III

THE INFLUENCE OF THE WOMAN QUESTION UPON SINGLE WOMEN

THE following comparisons between the life of women, especially their spiritual life of about fifty years ago and their life as it has shaped itself under the influence of the woman movement, have been arranged in *descending* scale. They begin with that phase of women's life in which this influence was most favourable from the point of view of life enhancement, namely with the life of *unmarried* women.

You will find to-day, among women seventy or eighty years of age, one or another type of that fine culture which the gifted single woman, in comfortable circumstances, could attain in the previous century. Her home, especially if it was an estate in the country, became a cultural fireside which radiated light and heat for relatives and friends. The lesser gifted disseminated, each according to her nature, comfort or discomfort, yet could in extremity at least be sure of the homage of their future heirs. Toward those dependent upon them, these women were sometimes kind, sometimes indifferent, sometimes hard: the feeling of social responsibility was an unknown idea to them. The *penniless* single women, on the contrary, were found either in one of the "respectable" positions which, however, brought with them a multitude of humiliations: as governess, companion, housekeeper—in Germany also as maid of honour at one of the numerous small courts—or in some charitable institution for gentle folks, an asylum for *pauvres honteuses*; but most frequently in the corner of the home of a relative. This corner was at times the warmest and most confidential in the whole house, that corner which the children sought for stories and sweetmeats; the youth, to find an embrace in which he could pour forth his grief, an ear which listened to his most beautiful dreams. But it happened more frequently that the "aunt," looked upon as a "necessary evil" was in reality that very thing. Humiliated and embittered, she became ingenious in making those about her suffer for her afflictions. Before they became hopelessly old, the "aunts" were the laughing stock of the young through their efforts, in the eleventh hour, to reach the "peaceful haven of matrimony"; and they themselves looked with envious eyes upon the good fortune of the young. We meet the unmarried woman of that time at her best as trusty servant who shared the cares, the joys, and the sorrows of the family and, in her garret chamber, of which she could be certain to the day of her death, she looked back upon a rich life lived vicariously. Not infrequently, she rejected a marriage proposal in order to stay with her beloved master and mistress to whom she knew she was indispensable. The superfluous women previously mentioned would have thrown themselves into the arms of Beelzebub had he come as suitor. When the years passed, when neither their desire for activity nor the thirst of the heart nor of the senses was quenched, then not infrequently insanity conjured up for these lonely women a life content for which they had longed in vain. To-day, however, we have for the position which the expression, "a forsaken old maid," betokens an entirely new type: "the glorified spinster," as the joyous, active, independent unmarried woman is called by the people among whom she first became a reality. Among these women, independent through their work, useful to society, that older type is still occasionally found perhaps, a survival of the time when emancipation was rather generally interpreted as freedom for masculinity. The "man-woman" in masculine attire, with weapons of defence against man in one hand and a cigarette in the other, her soul filled with mad ambition for her own sex and, as representative of her entire sex, with hatred toward the other, was however always rare. Now, she has almost entirely vanished, except alas, the cigarette. But she smokes it now often with—masculine friends! She follows in her mode of life, as in her dress, the law of good taste—not to offend; she endeavours, if only with a flower or two, to give a glimmer of cosy comfort to her place of work. This comfort, which often comes into the public life with woman is perhaps the reason why many men, who first looked with indignation upon feminine fellow-workmen, would now miss them. The more personal the culture of these women becomes, the more they endeavour, according to their time and means, to express their personality in the lines and colours of their dress and in the arrangement of their room. Those best situated often succeed, toward the end of their working days, in winning their own little home which they perhaps share with a friend, or they join a co-operative enterprise and can thus raise their standard of living. The same women who, at twenty-five, scornfully declared that they "would never bury their head in a sauce-pan," are now, at fifty, consciously aware of the significance of the table for the activity of the brain; indeed they are now quite as proud if they have prepared a good dish as they were in their youth when they passed a fine examination!

It is not to be wondered at that the emancipated women, exactly as all recently emancipated masculine classes and races, at first groped insecurely after a new form. The astonishing thing, on the contrary, is that women adapted themselves so quickly to the new circumstances; that the transition period furnished so few grotesque types;

that the present shows so many harmonious types, each in her own way. This harmony of single women is no mere form. It has its inner counterpart in the satisfaction with their existence, an existence in accord with their desires. The psychology was not exhaustive which saw in feminism only a "spinster question," a question of the unmarried woman, springing from the surplus of women and the increasing difficulty or disinclination of men to contract marriage—a question therefore for the ugly, not for the beautiful; for the unmarried, not for the married; for the poor, not for the rich. For a great number of beautiful women prefer to remain unmarried; a great number of rich desire to work; a great number of married women are zealous suffragists. Fifty years ago, we saw the most clever women idealise an ape into a god; now, the modern, intelligent working girl, when she looks about her for her ideal, exercises a lively criticism. She often flirts with one who exhibits some phase of the ideal, but she has too clear an understanding and too much to do to *imagine* a great feeling for one who is unworthy. So it often happens that youth has passed without such a feeling having stirred her. And she enters without deep regret the age when ambition and desire for power become her life stimulants. From these women of predominating mind and will is formed more and more what Ferrero calls "The third sex," Maudsley, "The sexless ant": energetic, clever, happy in their work, cool, but sound; in private life, in the zeal of everyday work, often egoistic but willing to make sacrifices in face of social exigencies.

So a great part of the fifty-year-old women form an exception since they with true instinct have remained unmarried. For in the same degree that their metallic being is well adapted to the machinery of society, it is little qualified to make a home for husband and children. They do not depreciate however the value of this task, unless they be fanatic feminists. In that event they reproach the women who wish to marry with "betraying the woman cause"; they demand at times, as imperative loyalty toward this cause, that their friends shall protest against the present marriage laws at least by the form of their marriage alliance if not even by not marrying at all. Their theory of equality has at times been carried so far that—as recently happened in France—they advocate women's performing also masculine military service.

But in spite of their aridity and inflexibility of principle how much more human are even *these* feminists than the "ill-natured" aunts of earlier times who became ill-natured exactly because their temperament was of the kind mentioned above, but who could find no sphere of operation for their passionate longing for activity. One or another was perhaps burning with ambition. For there are women as well as men who can live only as pagan gods, in the blaze and perfume of sacrificial fires. In their youth these ambitious natures could be satisfied by triumphs in social life. But later the passion became a fire in a powder cask and occasioned incessant explosions. Now it is the electric motive power for an activity of general utility. The "aunts" of the earlier time who felt themselves always overlooked and injured are most easily recognised again in the literary and artistic field to which daily bread or ambition now urges many women, who endeavour to compensate by energetic work for the talent which nature denied them. Since these women are ordinarily not people of understanding but of feeling, they must in a double sense be dissatisfied with a life which in addition is, in most cases, still filled with economic cares and the humiliations arising therefrom. And yet in spite of all, how much richer is their life to-day than it would have been fifty years ago when they would have been obliged to sit and draw their needles through interminable pieces of handwork, after ugly patterns and for unnecessary uses, or to compose sentimental birthday verses for persons whom they abominated.

Yet there are always those women natures who, in the past, had the qualifications for a real "dear aunt," who gently calmed the conflicts and filled the gaps in the home of which they had become members. The most tender and sensitive of these modern women, who, rain or shine, year in year out, hasten to and from a work indifferent to them at heart, not infrequently breathe a sigh of longing for those times when, as "aunts," they could have received and imparted warmth in a home. But then again there come moments when they know how to value the independence which puts them in a position to give help where otherwise there would be none; when for example they can send a nephew to college, or a friend to a sanatarium, or provide their mother with a nurse, which they themselves can not be.

This kind of single woman fulfills more or less the office of family provider just as she also is always ready with word and deed in circles of friends and comrades. These women are so engrossed that the time of love, sometimes love itself, passes them by without their observing it. Their youth flees and they feel with sadness that their woman's life is unlived. But they persuade themselves that they have had enough in their work, that many little joys can take the place of great happiness. And they believe this as truly as the infant believes he is satisfied when he sucks his own thumb. But some of these women acknowledge perhaps, when they have passed the fifties, that they were often tempted to call out to the first best man, "Give me a child." Sometimes it happens that in their last youth they appease their mother longing by adopting a foster child; sometimes they still this longing by a child of their own, from a love relation or a marriage. This late and uncertain happiness is often made possible exactly through their work. And then, if not earlier, they bless this work which gives them the economic possibility, and thereby also the courage, for this hazardous adventure.

More frequent than these are the cases however where single women, who have passed their first youth, find in friendship for another woman a valve for their, in great part, unused feelings. In some natures this friendship will be jealous and exacting, in others true and devoted. I wish to emphasise that I speak here of entirely *natural spiritual conditions*. There is to-day much talk about "Sapphic" women; and it is even possible that they exist in that impure form which men imagine. I have never met them, presumably because we rarely meet in life those with whom no fibre of our being has any affinity. But I have often observed that the spiritually refined women of our time, just as formerly the spiritually refined men of Hellas, find most easily in their own sex the qualities which set their spiritual life in the finest vibration of admiration, inspiration, sympathy and adoration.

. . . . . .

The fundamental types of single women depicted here—the person of intellect and the person of feeling—are found everywhere. The former according to current opinion already predominate in America; in Europe, it seems to me, the latter still prevail. That the main classes include innumerable varieties, it is needless to say. There are for example the numerous, quite ordinary, family girls who would be happy if they could give up their independence in order to enjoy the protection of their parents' or their own home. And the same obtains also with the quite as ancient type of woman, Undine, who—soulless and cold—enslaves all men. If she is in any civic vocation, she knows how to get the smallest amount of work for herself and, in case she is engaged in the artistic field, the best possible criticism. Conscience is an acquaintance which she has never made and she is also of the opinion that everything agreeable is permitted to her; she simply slides past anything disagreeable. Although work belongs to these disagreeable things, she continues it until she has found means to place her "qualities" in the most advantageous manner upon the matrimonial market.

The diametrical antithesis of this curvilinear type is the rectilinear. It has, just as the preceding type, existed at all times. It is the woman who really never demanded anything of life but "a work and a duty" and finds both in abundance in all positions of life. She is found year in year out at her desk, in appropriate working garb, free from all æsthetics; proud "if she never has needed to miss a day"; proud that she never has come late. On the contrary she never *goes* on time. For she has so grown into the business or the office that she takes everything upon herself that is required without murmuring, as a well-disciplined soldier in the ranks of the grey working army; thankful, in addition, if her long working cares yield her a little life annuity or pension for her old age. This type is found principally among women over fifty—fortunately. For this class of women which the pre-feministic circumstances created, have, by their "frugality" carried almost to the verge of criminality, by their humble, conscientious servitude, lowered the wages of their colleagues who are more full of life. These latter have begun work in the hope that it finally will "free" them; that is, will give them something of that for which their innermost being longs, not only their daily bread—a bread which sickness or a turn of affairs moreover can take from them at any time. And perhaps they never succeed even in having their own room where they at least could have repose! Underpaid, overworked, tired to death, who can wonder if these women have lost, if they ever possessed them, the essential characteristics of "womanhood"—active kindness, repose even in movement, charming gentleness? The Icelandic poet of yore already knew that "Few become fair through wounds." These women must put all their strength into their work and into the effort to conceal their underpayment by "respectable" clothing, or else lose their positions. In everything else they must economise to the utmost and perhaps in addition be laughed at because of their economy. They succeed, often admirably, in maintaining themselves in proud fair struggle, in rejecting "erotic" perquisites to add to their income and in fulfilling conscientiously the requirements of their work. Yet to do this with lively interest, with preserved spiritual elasticity, with quiet amiability—for this their strength does not suffice, exhausted by insufficient nourishment, insufficient sleep, still more insufficient recreation, and strained daily to the utmost. Their nervousness finds vent in either hard or hysterical expression and the public, annoyed by their ill-humour, divines little of the tragedies enacted in offices, business houses, cafés or similar places. If a suicide concludes the tragedy, the public shudders for a moment and—all goes on as before.

Thus "emancipation" presents itself in reality for millions of women. To what extent the middle-class woman movement is indirectly to blame for this fact has already been emphasised.

The essential reason is however the prevailing economic condition of society. By the uninterrupted fever of competition and the accumulation of riches, it dries up the soul and robs it of goodness as well as of joy. When the great, beautiful, eternal sources of joy are exhausted, the life stimulus is sought in exclusively physical pleasures, which are always made more exciting in order to be able to arouse still, in the languid nervous system, feelings of desire. Moreover, there is the neurosis and weariness of life of the overworked, of those continually quaking about their material safety, of those who *could* be revived by the noble and simple joys of life, to which those jaded with riches are already not susceptible; but for all these millions and millions such joys are not accessible because hunger for profit depresses wages. If in addition to that we take into account the increasing suffering of the best because of the ever developing feeling of solidarity; and if finally we consider that women, who through the protection of the home could preserve something of warmth-irradiating energy, are now in increasing numbers driven out of the home, then we have some of the reasons which—in higher degree than the religious and philosophic reasons which *also* exist—contribute to the joylessness of our time.

. . . .

A contribution to the meagre stock of good fortune of the present time is furnished however by the joy of life among young girls working under favourable conditions. Among them we meet a new soul condition, which could be designated, as briefly as possible, as *covetousness* of everything which can promote their personal development and a beautiful *liberality* with what is thus won. They can gratify their energetic desire for self-development by sport, travel, books, art and other means of culture; their freedom of action between working hours is not restricted by private duties. They can utilise their leisure time and their income as they please: for recreation, pleasure, social intercourse, social work or private, charitable activity. No father nor husband encroaches upon their free agency. And so dear does this liberty become to them through the manifold joys which it furnishes, that these young girls, in constantly increasing numbers, refuse to relinquish their individual independence for the sake of a marriage which, even presupposing the happiest love, always means a restriction of the freedom of movement that they enjoyed while single. And since the modern woman knows that, in the sphere of spiritual values, nothing can be attained without sacrifice, she prefers to keep free agency and to sacrifice love. If she chooses in the opposite direction, the task of adaptation will be the more difficult, the longer and the more intensely she has enjoyed freedom. The modern young girl, if she deigns to bestow her hand upon a man, not infrequently has her pretty head so crammed full of principles of equality that she sometimes (frequently in America), by written contract establishes her independence to the smallest detail, which sometimes includes separate apartments and the prohibition that either of the contracting parties shall have the key to the apartment of the other.

There are many varieties of the new type of woman. There is for instance the tom-boy, the "gamin," who for her life cannot give up the right to mad pranks and mischievous jokes. There is the girl consumed with ambition, who sacrifices all other values in order to attain the goal of her ambition in art or science. There is the fanatically altruistic girl, who considers the work for mankind so important that she feels she has not the right to an "egoistic" love happiness. There is the ascetic ethereal girl, who looks upon marriage and child-bearing as animal functions, unworthy of a spiritual being, but above all as *unbeautiful*. And for many of these modern, æsthetically refined, nervously sensitive young girls the æsthetic point of view is decisive. All love the work which permits them to live according to their ideals. Still it often happens that Ovidian metamorphoses take place: that the young girl sees the cloud or the swan transformed into a god, upon whose altar she sacrifices, with joy, her free agency and everything else which only a few weeks earlier she cherished as her holy of holies. The men who view this process with a smile, think that the anti-erotic ideals were only a new weapon of defence in the eternal war between the sexes. But these men often learn how mistaken they were when they themselves become participators in the war. They meet women so proud, so sensitive regarding their independence, so merciless in their strength, so easily wounded in their instincts, so zealous to devote themselves to their personal task, so determined to preserve their freedom, that erotic harmony seldom can be realised. Yes, these women often repudiate love only because it becomes a bond to their freedom, a hindrance to their work, a force for the bending of their will to another's will.

The women, womanly in their innermost depths,

who really feel free only when they give themselves wholly, are becoming continually more rare. But where such a wholly devoted woman still exists, she is the highest type of woman which any period has produced. Especially if she springs from a family of old culture. She has then, combined in her personality, the best of tradition and the best of the revolution evoked by the woman movement. The fibres of her being absorb their nourishment with instinctive certainty out of the fruitful soil which pride, devotion to duty, family love, requirements of culture and refinement of form, for many generations, have created. But her conscious soul-life flowers in the sun of the present; she thinks new thoughts and has new aims. Just as little as she disavows her desire for love, so little does she desire love under other conditions than those of spiritual unity and human equality. If she meets the man who can give her this and if she loves him, then he can be more certain than the man of any other time that he is really loved, that no ulterior motive obscures the devotion of this free woman. He has seen her susceptible to all the riches of life; has seen her assist in social tasks, perform the duty of every day joyful in her work, proud of her independence attained through her work. He knows that just as she is she would have continued to be if he had not entered into her life. How different is this girl from the one of earlier times, who was driven by the emptiness of her life into continual love affairs, which could not lead to a marriage nor exist in a marriage that possessed nothing of love!

This most beautiful new type of woman approaches spiritually the aforementioned type of single, aged women, who because of their economic independence found time for a fine personal culture. These followed not infrequently in their youth, from a distance it is true, but with joyous sympathy, the progress of the woman movement. They shook their heads later over its extremes. With new joy they regard the young girls just described, in whom they find a more universal development than in themselves, because these young girls have been developed through active consumption of power which was spared to the older women, although they must have summoned much *passive* energy in order to maintain their personality against convention. The young girls find often in these older women a fine understanding, which they richly reciprocate. Such terms of friendship are the most beautiful which the present has to offer: they resemble the meeting of the morning and evening red in the bright midsummer nights of the North.

No time could have been so rich in exquisite feminine personalities, at all ages and in all stages of life, as ours. We must not draw our conclusions regarding the abundance of such women, in the older culture epochs, from the illustrious names of women which incessantly recur in the pictures of the earlier times—like stage soldiers—until they give the illusion of a great host.

But exquisite women are even to-day exceptional. The Martha type rather than the Mary type predominates. This is due on one hand to decreasing piety, on the other hand to the kind of working and society life. Fifty years ago single women were often spiritually petrified, now more often they cannot succeed in settling into any form. Their existence, turned outwardly, widens their sphere of interest but makes their soul-life shallow. Restlessness is most unfavourable to the "development of the personality," which was however the goal of the emancipation of woman. This development is delayed mo t of all perhaps by the lack of personal contact with other personalities, of immediate, intimate human connections. This can, from no point of view, be supplied by the society or club life in which single women are to-day absorbed.

CHAPTER IV

THE INFLUENCE OF THE WOMAN MOVEMENT UPON THE DAUGHTERS

As late as sixty or seventy years ago, the daughters of good families had still few points of contact with life outside the four walls of the home. From the hands of nurse-maids they went into those of the governess, and after confirmation, studies were at an end. If it was a cultured home then reading aloud or music was often practised, whereby it is true no "specific education" qualifying them for examinations was attained, but frequently a fine universal human culture. There was always employment in the house for the zeal for work. The great presses were filled with linen which was not infrequently spun and woven by the daughters; in the autumn they assembled for sausage-making and candle dipping; later, for Christmas baking and roasting; in summer endless rows of glasses of preserves were set in the store-room. Before Christmas, night after night, Christmas presents were made; after Christmas, night after night, they danced. At these balls those in outer respects uncomely, received a foretaste of that waiting which must fill their life for many long years:

would the invitation to the dance—or the wooing respectively—come or not? Every man whose shadow merely fell upon the scene, was immediately considered from the point of view of a suitor. As the years went by the girl, who before twenty-five years of age was considered an "old maid," saw how the glance of the father and the brothers became gloomy, yes, she could even hear how "unfortunate" she was. If such a daughter lived in a home poor in books—and most of them were—then she could not even procure a book she wished. For the daughters worked year in year out without wages, in case they did not receive meagrely doled out pin-money which only through great ingenuity sufficed for their toilette. All year long there were christenings and birthday celebrations; in summer games were played, where it was possible riding parties arranged, in winter sleighing parties were organised. Other physical exercise was considered superfluous. The young girls were averse to going to a neighbouring estate if it lay a mile away; and during the week to take a long walk for pleasure or sit down with a book, which had been borrowed, would be considered simply as idling away one's time. In summer a cold bath was permissible—a warm bath was used only in cases of sickness—but swimming was considered so unwomanly, that whoever had learned it must keep it secret. Rowing, tobogganing and skating were, even if permitted in the country, yet half in discredit as "masculine."

When grandfather related an heroic deed of some ancestress whose proud countenance shone out among the family portraits, then the daughter of such a family must have asked herself why this deed was lauded while everything "manly" was forbidden her.

The days and years went by at the embroidery frame or netting needles, amid continuous chatter about the family and neighbours, amid eternal friction and in disputing back and forth over mere trifles. The confined nervous force sought an outlet, and in an existence where each one—according to the first paragraph of family rights—interfered in the greatest as in the smallest concerns of all the others, there was always plenty of material about which to become irritated and excited.

In the country, life was, however, fuller and fresher than in the city where the young girl had less to do and never dared go out alone; yes, where a walk was considered so superfluous, that the mother of the great Swedish feminist Fredrika Bremer advised her daughters to jump up and down behind a chair when they insisted that they needed exercise!

. . . . . .

The relation to the parents, even if the principle of unswerving and mute obedience was not wholly carried out, was ordinarily a reverential alienation. Neither side knew the inner life of the other. The temperament of the mother determined the everyday domestic comforts, the will of the father the external occurrences of life, from the trip to the ball to marriage. The daughter whose inclination corresponded with the will of the father considered herself fortunate. The one married against her will wept, but obeyed. As an almost fabulous occurrence it was related of one or another girl that she dared to say "No" before the marriage altar; cases were not unusual in which daughters received a box on the ear and were confined to their room until they accepted the bridegroom whom the father had chosen. Even if a mother, moved by the recollections of her own youth, attempted to support a daughter it rarely succeeded. For the power of the father rested quite as heavily upon the wife. But the worst however was to water myrtle year after year, without ever being able to cut it for a bridal wreath. Even she, who in her heart loved another, found it therefore often wisest to give her consent to an acceptable suitor. Only the one whose dowry was valued at a "ton of gold"—or who also was a celebrated beauty—could run the risk of declining a courtship; yes, she could permit herself to occasion it only to decline it. The more suitors she could recount, the prouder she was; such a beauty even embroidered around her bridal gown the monograms of all her earlier wooers.

The unmarried remained behind in an environment where the idea prevailed that "woman's politics are her toilettes, her republic is her household and literature belongs to her trinkets." The talented daughter sewed the fine starched shirts in which her stupid brother went to the academy and sighed therewith: "Ah, if one only were a man."

When the income of the house was small, she increased it perhaps by embroidery, sold in deepest secrecy; for it was a disgrace for a girl of good family to work for money. For her rebellious thoughts she had perhaps a girl friend to whom she could pour out her heart—or a sister. But it often fared with sisters growing old together, just as it must fare with North-pole explorers wintering together, that those holding together of necessity finally loathe one another from the bottom of their hearts. And yet the sisters were most fortunate who could grow old and die in their childhood home and were not compelled to become old household fixtures in the home of relatives.

Not infrequently this last fate was their portion because a father, a brother or a guardian out of personal, economical self-interest prevented their marriage, or a brother through debt or studies had defrauded them of their inheritance.

It was not the woman movement but the religious movement, beginning among the Northern peoples almost simultaneously with it, called in Sweden "Läseri" ("Reading") that was the first spiritual emancipation for the old or young unmarried girls—likewise for wives who longed for a deeper content. Because they took seriously the Bible doctrine that one should disregard the commands of the family in order to follow Christ, the home gradually became accustomed to one of the feminine members' going her own way. Often amid great struggles. For the "Reader" was more or less considered as insane; the father was ashamed of her, the mother mourned over her, the brothers laughed at her. But nothing could hinder those strong in their faith from following the inner voice. And so these women, without knowing it themselves, were a bridge to that emancipation of women to which they themselves later —Bible in hand—were often an obstacle.

. . . .

The movement *could* not however be prevented. And now—how is it now in the family? Already the ten-year-old talks about what she is sometime going to be. Now, the sisters go with the brothers to school or to the academy and share their intellectual interests as well as their life of sport. Now, the fathers and mothers sit at home often alone, for the daughters belong to that host of self-supporting girls who can gratify the parents by short visits only. Alas, these visits are not always an unclouded joy. There are collisions between the old and the young often over seeming bagatelles. But a feather shows which way the wind blows and the parents observe that, in the spiritual being of the daughter, the wind blows from an entirely different direction from theirs. The daughter, on the other hand, thinks that perfect calm prevails in the being of her parents; she wishes to raise the dust. The mother pleads her cause in dry and offended manner, the daughter in superior and impetuous words. Accustomed to her freedom, she encounters again at home control over her commissions and omissions, attempts upon her privacy from which she had been freed by leaving home. And they separate again each with a sigh that they "have had so little of one another." In other cases—when the parents have followed the times and the daughters understand that not only children but also parents must be educated with tenderness—then the visits to the parents' home become on both sides elevating episodes in their lives. The daughters repose in the parental tenderness, which they have only now learned to value when they compare it with their customary loneliness. The parents confide to the daughter their cares which she sometimes can effectively lighten, and they revive with her spiritual interests which they themselves had to lay aside. Through her own working life the daughter has gained an entirely new respect for her parents. Through her independence of parental authority she has now gained a frankness, which makes a real interchange of ideas possible. They discover that they can have something reciprocal for one another. The father, who perhaps at first sighed when the young faces vanished out of the home, now admits that it would have been foolish if the whole troop of girls had continued here at home and so had stood there at his demise, empty-handed, without professional training. The mother, who had helped them persuade the father, smiles, when he insists that he "would not exchange his capable girls for boys." And he is not at all afraid that the daughters could not marry if they would; he remembered indeed how his contemporaries declared that they "would never look at a girl student, a Blue stocking," and yet so many of these were now happily married to—girl students.

Beside these results of the independence of the daughters which elevate life for all sides, there are opposite cases; when, for example, a single daughter *without* outer economic compulsion or inner personal necessity, impelled only by the current of the time, leaves a home where her contribution of work could be significant, in order to follow a vocation outside. The results are often of doubtful value, not only from a social point of view but also from that of the family and herself, when the daughter remains at home but carries on a work outside. This comes partly because they are contented with less pay and thus lower the wages of those who support themselves entirely; partly because they over-exert themselves. In those cases where several daughters can share with one another the domestic duties, no over-exertion results perhaps. But when a single daughter combines an exacting professional work with quite as exacting household duties, then she is exhausted by her double task; then she feels the burden, not the joy, of work. For all professional working girls who remain at home, have moreover in addition, even under the most favorable circumstances, the spiritual strain of turning from work back again to the gregarious demands of the home, as well as to the many different attractions and repulsions, antipathies and sympathies which determine the deviations in temperature of the home; the strain of respecting the sensibilities which must be spared or of paying attention to the domestic demands which must be refused, if the work is not to suffer from lack of rest and time for preparation. All this can be so nerve racking that the young girl is seized with an irresistible longing for a little home of her own, where she would be mistress of her leisure time, and could see her own friends—not alone those of her family,—where she could join those who held the same views, where she, in a word, would live her life according to the dictates of her personal demands. If she can, she often does this. For to-day young girls *live to apply* the principle of the woman movement—individualism. The older women's rights advocates desired, it is true, that woman should be allowed to "develop her gifts," but she should "administer" them for the benefit of others; they desired that she should receive *new rights* from law and custom, but that she should seek always in *law and custom support and security for her action*. The young women's rights advocates, on the other hand, believe that their own growth, just as that of animals and trees, is intended above all for self-development, that in their own character the direction for their growth is specified, and that they have not the right to confine themselves by circumstances or subject themselves to influences by which they know they hinder the development of their powers, according to their individual natures. The more refined the feeling of personality becomes, the more exactly these young people understand how to choose what is essential for them and to repudiate what is a hindrance. But before they attain this certainty they evince often an unnecessary lack of consideration, and the family is often right when it speaks of the egoism of youth. They find no opportunity for helping father or mother nor for participation in the elders' interests. The whole family is rarely assembled even at meal-time; the daughters as well as the sons rush off to lectures, work, sport, clubs. The mother who sees how occupied the daughters are has not the heart to add to their work or to thwart them in their pleasures; thus she allows the selfishness of the young creatures to increase to the point where she herself in indignation begins—seasonably and unseasonably—to react against it. The young girl answers her mother's reproof then with the complaint that, "Mamma does not understand" her and that she is "behind her time." Especially the young examination-champions distinguish themselves by their arrogance in the family as in the club, where they look down upon the older ladies who have not passed examinations just as they do upon their own mother.

It fares best in the families, and they are even now numerous, where the mother herself has studied or worked outside the home and therefore knows what domestic services she may or may not require; where she herself personally understands the intellectual occupation of the young people and has preserved her own youthfulness, so that she becomes not infrequently the real friend of her daughters and sons. If the mother, on the contrary, was one of the many who, at the beginning of the woman movement, sacrificed her own talent to the wishes of her family or the demands of the home, in spite of the possibilities for its development made accessible to her at that time, then she has often absolutely no comprehension of the egoism of her daughter. She herself had acted so entirely differently! Or she understands fully that in her daughters as well as in her sons she views the attainment of a new conception of life, with all its Storm and Stress, which the spring-times in the life of mankind bring with them—an attainment in which, to her sorrow, she could not take part in her youth.

At such spring-times youth is not, as the parents hoped, sunlight and the twittering of birds in the home; but March storms and April clouds. The parents feel themselves at first swept out, superfluous, disillusioned. They are angered but rejuvenated, thanks to all the new points of view that youth makes valid. Yes, father and mother sometimes could live through a second youth if their own contemporaries did not depress their buoyancy by their disapproving astonishment and the children by their cool rejection of the comradeship of their parents. But in spite of this two-fold opposition, there are now fathers and mothers who are able to enjoy the riches of life quite as youthfully as and more deeply than their children; while the parents of earlier times, especially the mother, forever stagnated as early as forty. More and more frequently we find mothers who, like their daughters, lead a spiritually rich and emotional life, who have so preserved their physical youthfulness and who possess moreover through experience and self-culture so refined a soul-life, that, in regard to the impression they make, they are not infrequently the rivals of their daughters. They are already revelations of that type of woman which, in token of emancipation, has found the equilibrium between the old devoted ideal and the new self-assertive ideal. They view life from a height which gives them a survey also over the essential, in questions concerning their own children. Even if these become something other than the mothers wish, these mothers are so penetrated with the idea of individualism that they let the children follow their own course.

Modern fathers rarely find so happy a home as it once could be with a bevy of daughters always at hand. But they find the home richer in content, often also freer from petty dissensions. For in the measure in which *each* member of the family desires his right and his freedom, do all gradually learn to respect those of others. If the parents consider with dignity *their* right and *their* freedom, then a reciprocal consideration results after the boldness which youth evinces under the first influence of the intoxication of freedom. Youth, at first so proud and strong in their assurance of bringing new ideal values to life, begin themselves to experience how the world treats these; and what they once called their parents' prejudice appears to them now often in a new light. Their self-assertion becomes a product of culture, out of a raw material. The manifestations of their individualism become continually more discreet, more controlled, but at the same time more essential and more effective. When then the young people have found *their* way and the parents endeavour to turn them aside to the main road—which they call the way of wisdom or of duty—then certainly and with right the young people put themselves on the defensive.

Even a devoted daughter cannot bring to the home to-day as undivided a heart as formerly. But this gift was earlier a matter of course, so to speak, a natural result of the conditions. But if to-day a girl sacrifices a talent to filial duty, then it is an infinitely greater personal sacrifice; a real choice. And if she does not make the sacrifice, it is not in the least always on the ground of egoism. It happens often in conviction that the unconditional demand of Christianity that the strong must have consideration for the weak, makes these latter often egoists and tyrants; that the strong, who are more significant for the whole, are thus rendered inefficient.

If a troop of athletic boys continually conformed to the level of the weakest, then all would remain upon a lower plane, and the weak find no incentive to seek *their* triumphs in another sphere.

On the other hand it is fine and eminently sane and in harmony with the laws of spiritual growth, when the strong shall help the weak to reach a goal which is thus, in his own peculiar direction, really attainable by him. Neither paganism nor Christianity has created the most *beautiful* strength; it is a union of both. It has found its most perfect expression in art in Donatello's St. George, in Michelangelo's David: youths, whose victorious power conceals compassion and whose compassion embraces even the conquered: symbols of strength which has become kind, of kindness which has become strong. If a mother has seen this expression upon the face of her son or her daughter then she can address to life the words of Simeon: "Now let thy servant depart in peace for mine eyes have seen thy glory." For the glory of life is the harmony between its two fundamental powers— conquest and devotion: self-assertion and self-sacrifice. In every new phase of the ethical development of mankind the cultural problem is this harmony and the cultural profit is not the per-dominance of one of the two but the perfected synthesis of both.

This problem has now become actual, through the woman movement, for the feminine half of mankind, after the *unconditional* spirit of sacrifice has obtained for centuries as the indispensable attribute of womanliness. In the first stage of the woman movement the majority of the "emancipated" were still determined by their spirit of sacrifice, which they aspired to combine with their outside professional work. This generation lived *beyond its strength*. The younger generation of to-day does not believe that God gives unlimited strength. For they have seen that those who live unceasingly beyond their strength finally have no strength left, either for others or for themselves. And they know that in the long run one can live only upon his own resources and these must be conserved and renewed in order to suffice. But this knowledge makes the problem, which in the course of days and years appears in manifold different forms, only more difficult of solution: the problem to find the right choice in the collision between family duties, duties toward oneself and duties toward society; the choice which shall bring with it the essential enhancement of life.

The conflict is thus solved by some feminists: everything called family ties and family feeling is referred to the "impersonal" instinctive life, while our "personality" expresses itself in intellectual activity, in study, in creation, in universally human ends, in social activity, etc. And since the principle of emancipation is certainly the freeing of the "personality," it follows from this idea, in connection with *this definition of the personality*, that the liberated personality must place the obligations of the intellectual life absolutely above those of the family life; the outside professional work above the work in the home. In a word, the earlier definition of *womanliness* ignored the *universal human* element, the present definition of *personality* ignores the *womanly* element in woman's being. The last solution of the problem is quite as one-sided as the first.

The "principle of personality," as it has just been described is entertained especially in America. In Europe there are still women who reflect deeply upon their own being and—who have a depth over which they may meditate! These women have not yet succeeded in simplifying the problem which is the central one of their life. They know that not only do instincts, impulses of the will, feelings, form the strongest part of the individual character which nature has given them, but also that this part determines their thinking and creating power —their whole conscious existence. They know that their character receives its peculiarities through the development which they themselves accord to one or another side of their individual temperament. In one personality the intellectual life will predominate, in another the emotional: in one the ethical, in another the æsthetic motive.

The personality becomes harmonious only when no essential motive is lacking, when all attain a certain degree of development, a harmony which is as yet only so won that no motive receives its *greatest possible development.* Such a harmony has long been the especial characteristic of the most beautiful womanhood, while the most significant men have ordinarily achieved their superior strength in *one* direction, at the cost of harmony in the whole. If now women believe that they can achieve the strength of men without, for that reason, being obliged to sacrifice something of their harmony, then they believe their sex capable of possibilities which thus far have been granted rarely and then only to the exceptional in both sexes. What experience shows is: the greater harmony of single women in a *limited* existence as compared with the lack of harmony in the lives of daughters, owing to the irreconcilable problems which their *richer* existence brings with it. For these problems must be solved, at one time, by sacrifice of intellectual, at another, by sacrifice of emotional values. In every case, the sacrifice leaves behind it, not the joyful peace of fulfilled duty, but the gnawing unrest of a duty still ever unfulfilled. Every woman who has a heart knows it is at least quite as important a part of her personality as her passion for science perhaps. If for example she is obliged to surrender to another the loving service of a sick father in order to pursue scientific researches, then her heart is quite as certainly in the sick-room as, in case of the opposite choice, her thoughts would have been in the laboratory. By calling one factor "instinct" and the other "personality," nothing is in reality gained. Theorising ladies can easily write—the paper is forbearing. But human nature is of flesh and blood. And therefore thousands of women grapple to-day with tormenting questions:—When we women shall belong entirely to industrial work and to the social life, who then is left for the work of love? Only paid hands. What becomes then of the warmth in human life when such a division of labour is established that kindness becomes a profession, and the rest of us shall be exempt from its practice because our "Personality" has more important fields for the exercise of its strength? What does it signify to live for society when we come to the service of society with chilled hearts? If the warmth is to be preserved then we must have leisure for love in private life, a right to love, peace and means for love. Only thus can our hearts remain warm for the social life. Can the whole really profit if we sacrifice unconditionally that part of the whole which is nearest us? Can our feeling of solidarity increase toward mankind when we pass by exactly those people to whom we could, by our deeds, really show our sympathetic fellow-feeling?

The woman whose instinct life is still strong and sound, whose personality has its roots deep in life—which means not social life alone—she also understands how to determine what life in its deepest import purposes with her; she knows how she serves it best, whether by remaining in a position where she fulfils her personal obligations as part of a family or by seeking another position where she fulfils this obligation as a member of society.

It is true the erroneouus idea still prevails in many homes that the daughter must willingly sacrifice her social task for the family, a sacrifice which the family would never even wish on the part of a son. But the assurance that the daughter *could* have made another choice instils in the family, unconsciously, a new conception of her sacrifice, and gives to herself the courage to assume a position in the home other than that she held at the time when no choice remained to her. If the total of efficacious daughterly love of to-day and earlier times be estimated, this total would not prove less now. But it is now given rather in a great sum; earlier, on the contrary, in many small coins. Because of the professional work of the daughter, there are now often lacking in the home the ready obliging young hands whose help father and brother so willingly engrossed; the cheerful comforter, the admiring listener. But in a great hour the daughter or sister gives now often a hundred times more in deep, personal understanding. One draws a false conclusion when one thinks that the more closely a family holds together the more it signifies a corresponding unity and devotion.

The young act in submission because they permit themselves to be cowed by the family authority which like a steam-roller passed over their wills and their hearts. But the indignation that they experienced in their innermost hearts, the criticism which they exercised among one another, were not less bitter than that which they to-day openly utter.

The home life of fifty years ago was a school of diplomacy; it especially served to oppose cunning to the father's authority, and the mother often taught the children to use this weapon of weakness. Now the father does not wish to make himself ridiculous by saying: "I forbid you," for the daughter answers: "Well, then, I will wait until I am twenty-one." The threat, "I disinherit you," recoils from the determination of the daughter, "I can work." Only in a distant province, in a little town, or among the "upper ten thousand" of a large city, where the daughters still often receive a "general education," which does not fit them to earn their living, are they occupied all day without the feeling of having worked. They serve at five o'clock teas, embroider for charity bazaars, etc. But they also experience the power of the spirit of the time strongly enough to know that they lead a selfish life but not a life of self. The lower the scale of riches the more housework do the daughters have to perform. But as a result of the patriarchal organisation of labour they still perform this without their own responsibility, without the joy of independence, without regular unoccupied time and without one penny at their disposal!

Even in these circles however the spirit of the time is active; such a daughter leads now in every case a life of much richer content than some decades ago, when even though middle-aged she was still treated as ignorant innocence and must allow herself to be extolled to every possible marriage candidate. She suffers when she sees her mother as the submissive wife, whose continual according smile has graven lines of humility about her mouth, whose continually pacifying tone has made her voice whining. She suffers when the father cuts short a diversity of opinion with the words, "You have heard what I said—That will do." She suffers when her brothers find her "insufferably important" or declare her new ideas "crazy." But exactly these new ideas about the right and freedom of woman, which she encounters everywhere, have given a dignity to her own being which has its influence even without words. On the other hand, the fact that the fathers lose one legal right after another over the feminine members of the family has its effect, so that they gradually change their tone, the clenched fist falls less and less frequently upon the table, the disdain is silenced, and even in the provinces the family life is changing more and more from the despotic political constitution to the democratic, where each one maintains his position by virtue of his own personality. There are still men it is true, who wish to confine "woman's sphere" to the four "C's"—"Cooking, clothing, children, church." But there is no one who now insists that "a girl *cannot* learn Mathematics," or that it is "unwomanly to pore over books"—sayings which were still often heard fifty years ago. Certainly there are still men who accept the cherishing thoughtful care on the part of the women members of the family as obvious homage. But the men are becoming more and more numerous who receive these womanly acts of tenderness with waking joy. Daughters and sisters of earlier times have pardoned the vices of their fathers and brothers seven and seventy times; those of the present throw away the fragments of trust and love which have been irrevocably shattered. The assurance that the daughters and sisters could do nothing else except pardon, since they were dependent upon their tormentors, often made the fathers and brothers of earlier times grossly inconsiderate. The men of to-day will be refined by the necessity of showing consideration and justice to their daughters and sisters if they wish to enjoy their presence in the home. Fathers and brothers have, in a word, gained quite as much spiritually through the loss of their power to oppress as the daughters and sisters have gained in being no longer oppressed. And this experience will be repeated in marriage when man and wife shall be absolutely free and equal.

CHAPTER V

THE INFLUENCE OF THE WOMAN MOVEMENT UPON MEN AND WOMEN IN GENERAL

In their struggle for freedom for the same opportunities of study, for the same fields of work, the same citizenship as man, women have encountered all possible opposition, from that of the Pope, who recently pronounced the most positive condemnation of the whole movement for the emancipation of woman, and that of Parliament, to the rough pranks of students. Man's attempt to define the boundaries of "woman's natural sphere" continues always. The woman physician, for example, had to struggle, in her student years, against prejudice in the dissecting room, and, in her practice, against the professional jealousy of men. The history of emancipation has much shameful conduct on the part of man toward woman to record. Great reluctance to recognise the results of woman's work is still common. When this work, in literature and art for instance, is compared with man's, the comparison is made not for the purpose of getting a finer understanding of woman's peculiar characteristics, but only to disparage it. The energy which men of the present time not infrequently lack they cannot endure to recognise in women, who often possess it in high degree. In the Romance countries, self-supporting working women are always looked upon as a special caste—a caste into which a man does not marry however high respect he pays, theoretically, to "les vierges fortes."

And yet how different—and more beautiful—are the present relations between men and women in general, especially among the Germanic peoples. A friendly comradeship prevails among the young men and women studying at the university, in art academies, music schools, business colleges, etc. In the North, this comradeship often continues from the primary schools, through the grades to the university, with results advantageous to both sexes. Especially in the years under twenty, this comradeship has a significance which cannot be overestimated. Girls, who were, earlier, confined to a narrow, uninteresting, joyless family circle, now often find in the circle of masculine and feminine comrades their share of the joy of youth without which life has no springtime. Youths who formerly had known no other young women than those with whom they should never have come in contact, now learn to know soulful, pure-minded girls, and this gives them a new conception of woman. Both sexes now experience together the joys of youth in such fresh and significant forms as folk-dancing, sport, etc. They have opportunity for stimulating interchange of ideas in a great circle, and quiet discussion with a few congenial friends. During the last twenty or thirty years, young men and young women have again begun to discover one another spiritually, discoveries which since the days of romanticism have been made only through the stained glass of literature. In the romantic period, men and women exercised reciprocally upon one another a humanising influence. A like influence again obtains at the present time, but upon a much broader basis. The men and women of romanticism formed a group bound together only by spiritual relationship, in which the women aspired to the culture of the men and shared their intellectual interests, while the men promoted the women's "desire for men's culture, art, knowledge, and distinction" (*Geluste nach der Männer Bildung, Kunst, Weisheit und Ehre.*—Schleiermacher). Now, young people studying in different fields exert a mutual humanising influence and thereby learn to know one another from the side of intelligence as well as from that of character and disposition. Thus are dispelled certain illusions and conceptions almost forced upon them through which both sexes in the years of adolescence once regarded each other. Men as well as women obtain a finer criterion for the conception of "womanliness" and of "manliness"; both discover the innumerable shadings which these conceptions conceal; both recognise that the sexes can meet not only upon the erotic plane, but upon a plane that is universally human; finally, both learn that the more perfect and complete human beings they become, the more they have to thank one another for it.

Comprehension in erotic relations is most difficult because, there, women are far in advance of men. Woman's ideal of love, however, is becoming more and more the ideal of young men. Young girls, on their side, are beginning to understand better the sexual nature of men. The whole world in which man received his culture, won his victories, suffered his defeats, is no longer *terra incognita* to women; they have lost the blind reverence or the blind hostility with which they formerly regarded the doings and dealings of men. Men, on the other hand, are learning that the domestic labours for the comfort of the family, which they have thus far regarded as the sole duty of woman, cannot engross her whole soul, that domesticity leaves many wishes unfulfilled. So both sexes have begun, each on its own side, to build a bridge across the chasm which law and custom had dug between them. The young still ponder over the enigmatical antitheses in their natures, yet they find they have very much that is human in common with one another. In comradeship, however, that "chivalry" vanishes, which among other things consisted in the ideal that the young men had always to bear all the burdens and duties. Now as a rule, the girl carries her own knapsack on excursions and pays her share of the expenses.

But if she really needs help, the youth is quite as ready as before to grant it to her, just as she also on her part is ready to assist according to her strength: honest friendship has replaced rapturous chivalry. This friendly comradeship often satisfies the young man's need of feminine kindness and enjoyment in those dangerous years when, as a young man said, "Three fourths of the life of a youth, conscious and unconscious, is sex life." And nothing can more effectually prevent him from degrading himself than access to a circle where in quiet and freedom he meets young girls, without an indelicate, intruding family surveillance, interfering and asking him about his "intentions." If between two such comrades an erotic feeling finally develops, even if the wooing takes place in a laboratory instead of a romantic arbour, the possibilities always exist, in the golden haze of love, of making mistakes. But both have, however, had opportunities of seeing each other in many character-illuminating situations; they have observed each other, not only with their own eyes, but also through the more critical glasses of the comrade circle. On the other hand, it often happens that discussions and interchange of letters conjure up a congeniality which exists only in opinions and temperament, not in nature. It is fortunate when this is discovered in time. Otherwise bitter conflicts may be the result, should a strong individual nature wish to mould the other after himself or after his ideal of man or woman.

For that anyone loves the individuality of another without illusions is still very rarely the case. It now happens somewhat more frequently, since young people in comradeship learn to know mutually their ideals and dreams, as well in erotic as in universally human aspects. But if these ideals and dreams do give a hint of character, comradeship brings a true knowledge of character only when it also offers an opportunity of seeing others *act;* not only of *hearing* them speak of themselves. Such analyses of one's own soul or the soul of others in the atmosphere of tea and cigarettes, music and poetry, give the "interesting" masculine or feminine parasites opportunity to ensnare a victim, who is then intellectually or erotically, often even economically, sucked dry.

But even if such an interchange of ideas really enriched all, it can be carried to excess and become deleterious to energy for work, directness, and idealism. However beneficial may be the honesty of to-day in sexual questions, the discussion of the instincts of life which has now become a commonplace is also dangerous. These discussions are fraught with the same danger to the roots of human life as is a continual digging up of the roots of a plant to see how it is growing.

The earlier a marriage can be consummated, the less is the danger of freshness being lost in this way; the greater the prospect that man and wife will grow close together, just as do the man and wife of the people, through the difficulty of the common struggle for existence. But if this struggle becomes easier before youth has entirely passed, then there enters often into the life of the man a crisis which the practised French call "La maladie de quarante ans": the need of the man for a new erotic experience. While those on a lower erotic plane, to-day as at all times, seek this in transient secret alliances, it leads those on a higher level in our time to the most tragic of all separations, where the man—after decades of the most intimate life together, of the most faithful work together, of mutual understanding—drives the wife out of the home in order to bring in a young wife who has never been to him, perhaps never can be to him, a fellow fighter and helper, as the repudiated wife was, but who has for him the charm of the mystery which the maiden had for the man before the days of coëducation, sexual discussions, comradeship, and dress-reform!

Women students now escape the earlier danger of the daughter of the family, falling in love out of lack of occupation. They have not the time, often also not the means to permit themselves erotic dreams. There are among them many poor girls who dare lose no single semester, for they must hasten to earn their livelihood. Moreover, such a girl knows that if she should yield to the need for tenderness, for support, that is so strong in her, the same fate could happen to her as to this or that fellow student who after a short happiness was left alone when the lover found a good match. And she was left behind not only in her sorrow but also in her work. And the more a yearning girl buries herself in her studies, the more science or art unlock their riches to her, the happier, more full of life she feels herself in spite of loneliness, scanty means, and shabby dress.

Among women students there are also many of the cerebral type, mentioned above, women who need tenderness neither in the form of friendship nor of love; yes, who fear in both a bond for their "free individuality." These take part in sports, discuss, jest, with their fellow men students, openhearted and unconcerned, without thinking whether they please or not. All these young girls now go about with perfect freedom; even in the Romance countries, a young woman can now go alone with her bag of books or her racquet. For in circles where study has not yet exercised its freeing influence, sport has brought this about.

In America, student life, because of the early entrance of the men into the professions, becomes more a one-sided, feminine comrade-life. There, the women have to develop their arts of the toilet for each other, whom they find more interesting, more worthy of pleasing than the masculine sex. Even in Europe, feminine comradeship in the student years is at times most intimate. For a friendship between a young girl and a young man often ends with love—on one side. Or in an intimate circle A has fallen in love with B, but B with C, etc. Such eventualities the wise girl will avoid for they can bring both suffering and obstruction to her work. With women comrades, she has, without this risk, an interchange of ideas which promotes study, deepens culture, opens up new views, and gives to all new impulses. There exists, at least at the present time, a difference between the masculine and feminine method of inquiry, of solving problems, of apprehending ideas, which results in the fact that comradeship between women cannot take the place of comradeship between men and women. It is, however, for deep and beautiful natures often impossible at the beginning of life to be capable, in a spiritual sense, of more than a single friendship with their own sex; for each new spiritual contact becomes a new and difficult problem. For such men or women a friendship with a comrade of their own sex is often the richest advantage of their student time. Often a student in good circumstances finds her joy in taking care of some lonely comrades. They find at her apartments, in a friendly welcome, a few flowers and pictures, a teakettle, a fireplace, that feeling of homely warmth for which the shivering students have longed,—a longing which has often driven a lonely, impressionable youth from the dreary students' room to "rough pleasures." Now when he leaves the little comrade circle, his sweetest memories of home, his finest dreams, vibrate in him. And the timid girl goes in the certainty that there is another girl who is concerned about her wretched fate.

In such a quiet as also in a more lively comrade-life both sexes learn to know not only each other but also different classes and, in certain European universities, the several nations. It is not unusual for nine or ten races to be found represented in one small group of comrades. Life thus becomes everywhere enriched by strong manifestations or fine shades of congeniality; spiritual attractions and repulsions cross one another; inspiring or restraining impressions radiate in all directions. It would be quite as impossible to estimate the fructifying influence of such a friendly intercourse as to measure the life which comes into existence on a spring day filled with the sigh of the wind, the fluttering of butterflies, and humming of bees.

In such a circle of comrades, devotion and capacity for sacrifice are past belief, especially in the nation where "the girls wear short hair and the young men long hair," as a wag characterised the young Russians studying abroad. That a couple of Russian girls, for a whole winter, possessed together but a single pair of shoes and so could never go out at the same time, is one of the innumerable small and great expressions of the feeling of solidarity among the poorest students of the university.

When the comrade life assumed the form exclusively of coffee-house visits, then the women had to revolt against it. But they often, alas, allowed themselves to be carried with the stream. Because the coffee-house life at first really gave a certain polish to the intelligence, it could for a short time have its justification. But when a blade is worn out, the artist of life should cease grinding; if on the contrary he allows the grindstone to go on continually, then at last he has only the haft in his hand. Formerly, it was only the young men but now even the girls wear out thus their weapons or tools before they ever use them seriously.

The darkest side of coëducational life has been that women could demonstrate their equal capability with men in no other way than by the same courses and examinations as those of the men. The eagerness of women to prove their like proficiency with men in study and in sport has often had disastrous physical results. These are continually becoming more infrequent, thanks to the decreasing prudery in regard to the sexual functions and to the increasing hygienic conscience. The intellectual results, however, continue to exist and are disastrous alike for both sexes; but because of the ambition and conscientiousness of girls, perhaps still more disastrous for them. The examinations which they pass are often dearly bought. This was not noticed in the beginning, when a woman doctor was still looked at with wonder as a noteworthy product of culture, and regarded herself also with wonder. Truly she had sacrificed to grinding and cramming for examinations a multitude of youthful joys, but she had, as was thought, won in this way much greater values. This, however, is not always really the case.

Ethically, the conscientious girl is certainly above the boy who, not infrequently in the unconscious instinct of self-preservation, idles away his time. But the mental strength of the latter may frequently be better preserved in any determined direction. Girls, conscientious and zealous in their work, have filled their heads full of lessons to which the coming examination and not their own choice has urged them. What is thus crammed in is not assimilated and consequently has not promoted spiritual or mental growth. But it has taken up room and has thereby impaired the intellectual freedom of motion and compelled the natural individuality to compress itself so that it is long before the space conditions in the brain permit it to extend again—in case it is not simply choked by all the chaotic mass that has been absorbed. How many young girls have come to the university or to the art academy full of thirst for knowledge and energy for work! But after a few years they feel the disgust of surfeit, unless they have found a teacher who has been to them a leader to the essentials in science or in art. Then their joy in study could really be as rich as they had once dreamed it—yes, as perhaps even their grandmothers had dreamed it when they had to content themselves with their little text-books written for "girls." Many young girls maintain to-day, through some teacher or some masculine comrade, that spiritual development which only an exceptional relationship between a father and daughter, a brother and sister, could give in earlier times.

When men and women can study together, then the relationship later between masculine and feminine fellow workmen will, as a rule, be better than when the sexes work independently in the student days. It is true masculine competitors still have recourse to the weapon of spreading reports of the incapacity of their feminine competitors —at times honestly convinced of it themselves. The same weapon is of course turned also against masculine competitors. Yet there it is a question of the *individual*, while in regard to women, the *sex* is often the only proof the man thinks he need assign for the inferiority of their work. It can be said, however, upon the whole, that the relationship between men and women professional colleagues exhibits the same good side as the common student life, although naturally to a lesser degree. The joint work does not often leave much time for significant interchange of ideas, and after working hours each usually longs for new faces. The influence of joint labour is often limited to the refining effect that the presence of one sex exercises upon the other. Small services are mutually rendered and each worker learns also to respect the achievements of the other; or one is provoked because the work which should have been dispatched by the other now falls to his share!

If the woman performs the same work as the

man, then she is often indignant because she must do it for smaller compensation than he. All too easily, the feminists forget that this injustice is equalised if a man who wishes to establish a family cannot obtain a post which he seeks because a woman retains it who can be satisfied with a smaller wage since she remains in her parents' home. For this disparity, raising bitterness on both sides, there is no remedy under the present economic system. Feminists can *demand* the same compensation, but working women will not obtain it so long as the supply of workers is to the demand as one hundred to one in the professional occupations to which women flock. In vain underpaid women will call to the agitators of the woman movement, "Help us to obtain endurable conditions of life." The only honest answer is, "Help one another, just as the working men have helped one another, by union and solidarity!"

The competition of the sexes in the labour field is only indirectly connected with the woman movement; it is a part of the social question and will therefore only be touched upon here.

The hostility which the competition between the sexes has evoked is a factor in the social war; and if—*by reason of this competition*—marriage decreases, then such competition is a form of social danger. If the cause is sought in the woman movement, then the question is begged completely, because the women with sufficient income *to be able* to live at home without industrial work, after the loss of a husband or a father, are constantly becoming more rare. There is the additional fact that in many positions where man and woman have equal salary, the woman is preferred because of her greater honesty and faithfulness to duty. Further it must be emphasised that, even in middle-class vocations, women with increasing frequency earn their *whole* livelihood, not merely a supplementary remuneration, when if they did not thus work they would be a burden to some man and so perhaps prevent him from marrying. Many of these women would wish nothing better than to enjoy the warmth of "the domestic hearth" to which men in theory relegate them; but since no man offers this warmth, they must at least be allowed to procure fuel for their lonely hearth fire.

When men declare that "the only duty which has life value for a woman is to be man's helpmeet," then they ought not to forget that this task is more and more rarely assigned to a woman, because men prefer to do without her aid, and even find a richer life in bachelorhood than in marriage. They should not dare to forget also that a great number of men disinclined or disqualified for work compel their sisters, daughters, wives, to undertake the task of family provider, and these women also must forego being, "in the quiet of the home, man's helpmeet."

However weak the feminist logic often may be, it is not so weak as the anti-feminist logic of man. Masculine vacuity has found there an arena where it performs the most incredible gymnastics. The hysteria of literary fanatics, the crude lordly instincts of the mediocre man, the irritation of the masculine good-for-nothing at the increasing ability of women, the rage, confounding cause and effect, over the competition of women—these are some of the reasons for the present antagonism between men and women. The deepest reason is this: the more woman is compelled to maintain the struggle for existence under the same social conditions as those under which men have been thus far compelled to struggle, the more she loses that character by which she gives happiness to man and receives it from him. A diminished erotic attraction is frequently the result, not of the work of women, but of their work under such conditions that the drudging, worn-out women comrades finally appear to their masculine colleagues only as "sexless ants." Sometimes they really exhibit that obliteration of all characteristic marks of sex which Meunier has indicated to us in his *Woman Miner*, a great thought-inspiring work of art.

Many a woman of the present time, deeply feminine, suffers under this compulsory neutralising of her womanly being. Others again consider this a path to complete humanity.

But the complete personality is only that man or woman who has cultivated and exercised the strength which he or she as a human being possessed without having neutralised thereby the characteristic of sex. It is tragic when nature herself creates deviations from normal sexuality, but criminal when the ideas of the time weaken sound instincts and inculcate unsound ones. It is not woman nature but the denatured woman who is beginning to grow through the ultra-feminism which looks down upon woman's normal sexual duty as only a low, animal function.

That sound men abominate this tendency is justifiable. On the other hand, it is unwarrantable to confuse a variation of feminism with the woman movement in its entirety, a movement which includes in itself a great earnest desire to work for the welfare of both mothers and children. As a manifestation of womanliness in its most complete, perfect form, many men still elect the woman whose entire life-content consists in the cult of her own beauty, a cult whose attendant phenomenon is the æsthetic culture which raises the temple about the altar. Under this perfect and apparently inspired form there is, however, rarely anything to be found of that which the man seeks: the longing and the power of true womanhood to give happiness by erotic and motherly devotion. Such women, like those cerebral women engrossed by their studies and their work, allow a real love to pass them by; men are only sacrificial servants of the cult, and the high priest is chosen not upon the ground of motives of feeling. This type is said to be more common in America than in Europe. But it existed thousands of years ago on the Tiber as well as on the Nile. That

Cleopatra in the language of feminism now speaks of the "right of the personality," and means thereby her right to represent no other value in life than that of the white peacock and the black orchid—the value of rarity—that does not make her a "product of the woman movement."

But certain men characterise a woman thus, if they have been deceived in her: a psychology which equals in value that of the feminist when she speaks of man as the "oppressor," the "corrupter,"—without noting that the world is full of poor men corrupted or tormented by women! Amid such mutual accusations, just or unjust—whereby *gifted* men maintain generalisations about "woman's" being which are quite as ingenuous as those which *silly* women propose about "man's" being—the sexes, in the days of the woman movement, have been almost as much alienated from each other as drawn together. The estrangement has taken place in the erotic field and through labour competition; the reconciliation has been effected—leaving out coëducation—by common industry and the social activity of both sexes.

The middle-class women of Europe have still so little share in the control of production that one cannot determine whether or not they have even awakened to the understanding that the fundamental condition of a universal life-enhancing issue of the woman movement must be new social conditions One cannot yet predicate anything at all in regard to their desires to promote more humane labour conditions and a more just distribution of profit. Under the system now prevailing they must, like men, either conform to it or be destroyed economically. It is even so in public offices and similar fields of labour. Just as so many young men do, at the beginning of their career, a great number of women attempt to abolish the abuses and mitigate the formalism. But they meet such obstacles that, like the young men, they are obliged to abandon the effort; or they are compelled to give up the position whereby they win their scanty bread.

In this way, principally, the work of women in the sphere of charitable activity has given to men the opportunity for a correct valuation of the social working power of woman. Men have then in a wider sphere than that of the family circle, so often overlooked by them, learned to appreciate feminine enthusiasm and capacity for organisation, energy and devotion, initiative and endurance. Innumerable men—from the soldiers up, who in the hospitals of the Crimea literally kissed Florence Nightingale's shadow on the floor of the hospital ward—have learned in the last half century that life has become more kindly for them since social motherliness has obtained for itself a certain elbow-room. The more women lose their present fear of appearing, in coöperation with men, "womanly" impulsive, savage in face of injustice and cruelty, the more will they signify in that joint work where, at least to-day, they still have a more fortunate hand—the hand of the mother.

And since a single fact is more convincing than a thousand words, so the facts gained in the social activity of woman have won, in later years, many men supporters of woman suffrage. The arguments derived from abstract right—however obvious they may be for every tax-paying, law-abiding woman—go to the rear to make way for the argument of "social utility."

Not only women themselves but men also refer now to what women have accomplished when they are allowed to work in the service of society; they point to the reforms which were retarded or bungled because women had no immediate influence there where appropriations were granted and laws were enacted.

Especially significant for the reconciliation of the sexes is the joint social work of young people. The temperance cause or the education of the masses or socialism now brings together a host of young men and girls, who learn thereby that the social as well as the private life of labour gains in strength and wealth if men and women participate in it together.

The men who fear political life for woman are, however, right. Just as this life has injured the best qualities in the manhood of many men, so will it impair the womanhood of many women. Neither the spiritual personality of woman nor of man, nor even their secondary physical sex characteristics can withstand the influences of their private *milieu*, of their private labour conditions. Why should women better resist the influences of the public life? When the man is compelled, in political work for the state, to neglect in the highest degree the foundation of the state —the home—how should women be able to do otherwise than the same thing? The political work of both can benefit the home *in general* but *their own* home must always suffer for it, for a time at least. Women will learn, as so many men have already learned, that the fresh enthusiasm, the unexhausted optimism with which they entered the political life soon vanish before party pressure, general prejudice, opportunism, and the demands of compromise. And just as now so many men for these reasons withdraw from Parliament, many women will do likewise when they learn that what they can accomplish there with the characteristics peculiar to them, is so insignificant that it does not compensate for the injury which ensues because these characteristics are missing in the home.

If the eligibility of woman is really to benefit society, then the right of resignation must be unconditioned for mothers, and they themselves must understand that the parliamentary mandate is incompatible with motherhood so long as the children are still in the home; in like manner during the same period, the franchise of the mother of a family must not result in rushing into electioneering. The ballot in and of itself does not injure the fineness of a woman's hand any more than a cooking receipt.

Because woman's motherhood must be preserved, if she is to bring to the social organism a really *new* factor, so she must always continue to be found and to work in private life, in order to be, meanwhile, useful in public life. The genius of social reform which women will develop can complement that of man only if this genius is of a new order; if it originates thoughts which bring new points of view to the social problems, wills which seek new means, souls which aspire to new ends. Women could, if they received their full civic right before they lost their intuitive and instinctive power through masculinisation, effect the progress of culture as, for example, the entrance of the Germans influenced the antique world.

The sooner woman receives her political franchise, the more, on the whole, can be expected from it. The generation which has now fought the fight for suffrage is wholly conscious of the reforms that await woman for their final realisation. And this generation of women would introduce into the political life a new, fresh current. In any event, we can hope to secure from women new impulses and better organisation in political life, as has already been the case in social life.

But every new generation of parliamentary women, who together with the men have been "politically trained," would have—as long as the present economic conditions obtain—continually greater economic interests to advocate "parliamentarily," and would also for other reasons evince the same parliamentary maladies as the men evince now. And as little as evil men lose their evil characteristics because of the franchise, quite as little will bad women lose theirs. The entrance of women into politics cannot therefore—as certain feminists maintain—signify the victory of the noble over the ignoble. But it signifies a great increase in noble as well as ignoble powers hitherto inactive in political life, which in the wider sphere that they there maintain oppose one another, now conquering, now yielding. Men and women *together*, however, will be able to enact more humane laws than men alone can enact. Questions concerning women and children can be treated with deeper seriousness by men and women *together* than is now the case. Men and women *together* will consider the social life from more significant points of view than can one sex alone. Government consisting of men and women *together* will be more profound than heretofore. No one who has observed the effects of masculine and feminine coöperation in fields already mentioned can doubt this. Who can deny that with the civic right of woman her feeling of social responsibility will increase and that her horizon will widen? And therewith her value as wife and mother of men will also increase? But she will increase in value for the men closely connected with her as well as in social respects. The woman of earlier times, for all of whom society might go to pieces if only *her* home and family prospered, was only in a restricted sense man's help. In certain great crises she usually betrayed him simply because she wholly lacked the social feeling.

Obviously, the female member of Parliament cannot confine herself solely to questions which concern the protection of the weaker and the education of the new race. The more women concentrate upon the cause of justice against power, and of public spirit against self-interest, the more advantageous it will be for her herself and for the public life. But concentration is, unfortunately, exactly what modern parliamentarism does not promote; what it does promote is disintegration.

Woman has, however, where she has entered into parliamentary life as elector and eligible, shown thus far exactly this tendency toward concentration. She has worked for moral, temperance, and hygienic questions; for questions concerning schools and education of the masses; for mother and child protection; reform of marriage laws, and kindred subjects. What thinking man can maintain that all this does not belong to "woman's sphere" or can say that these and similar social interests have been sufficiently attended to by an exclusively masculine government? Already the opposite danger appears in certain social spheres: an exclusively "feminine government."

In the present forms of public life, however, much feminine power will without doubt be wasted. Only when man, upon a higher plane, has created a new kind of representation "of the people," where professional interests in every sphere are represented, can the highest vocation of woman—motherhood—come into its rights.

It belongs to the necessary course of historical development that women also go through the stage of party-power politics in order together with man to reach the stage of social politics and finally that of culture politics.

But women cannot wait until this development has been attained; they must accomplish it together with man. Just as the best masculine powers sooner or later must be concentrated to transform increasingly untenable parliamentary conditions, so the best feminine powers will also work in the same direction, especially if the will becomes intense in mothers not only to awaken in their children the social spirit, but also to create for them better social conditions.

In later years, the movement for the suffrage of woman has not only filled the world with suffrage societies but the agitation has even achieved popular representation in eighteen European countries, in the legislative assemblies of a number of American States, in Australasia, in legislative assemblies in Canada and in the Philippines. In Iceland as well as in Italy, in Japan as in South Africa, the movement is in progress, and whoever thinks it will not attain its goal is politically blind.

When anti-feminist men prophesy that men will love their mothers, sisters, wives, and daughters less when pitted against them as political opponents or competitors, they prophesy certainly in many cases the truth. Politics have already estranged fathers from sons, brothers from brothers. But this demonstrates only either that the personal feelings were weaker than the political passions or that these latter have destroyed the attributes which made the personality lovable. But if men are really able to love and women remain lovable, even as political personalities, then a man will not cease to love a woman, even if she votes for a different congressional candidate! Such prophecies have not been verified in other spheres from which men sought to intimidate women by similar warnings. For woman retains her power over man if she retains her womanly charm, created out of peace, harmony, and kindness. Not that *of which* a woman speaks, not that *for which* she works, determines man's feeling and conduct; but *how* she does it. A woman may charm a man by a political speech, and drive him away by her table talk. A poor working woman can, without a word, induce the same man to give her his seat in a street car who the next minute can be brutal to an assuming and incapable fellow workwoman. In a word, what a woman makes of her rights and what they make of her—that alone determines the measure of veneration, sympathy, love, which she may expect from a man.

That women have lost their equilibrium cannot be denied. How could it be otherwise? Not only have they in the last half century experienced, together with man, Naturalism and the New Romantic movement, Neo-Kantianism, the Higher Criticism, Bismarck and Bebel, Darwin and Spencer, Wagner and Nietzsche, Ibsen and Tolstoi, Haeckel and von Hartmann, and still many, many more, but they themselves in dizzy haste have been hurled out of their position in society, protected by the family, which they had occupied for centuries. It is obvious that at the present moment the spiritual mobility of women must be greater than their harmony; that the raw culture material which they possess must be richer than that which they can utilise; their life experiences more significant than their art of life. The modern woman must appear for the present less symmetrical, more uncertain, than man's ideal woman in earlier times. But enduring cultural progress cannot be measured by comparison with the ideal figures of the poetry or of the life of earlier times. It must be estimated according to the *average type* in a certain period. And the average woman of our time is, in the fullest significance of the word, more full of vitality and adaptability, more individually developed, more beneficial socially, than the average woman of fifty years ago. With the freedom of movement the social feeling has increased; with the participation in universal human culture, the richness of content: the spiritual life has become more complex, and the possibilities of expression of this new soul-life, more numerous.

But since the average man, in the meantime, has undergone no comparable development, he is estranged, has lost his bearings, and consequently repudiates a movement which, directly and indirectly, makes such great demands for the development of his own higher spiritual qualities. Heretofore men could force women to endure undue interference, and so have deprived them of the education wherein the possible consequences of action are considered at the same time with the thought of the action. But the woman movement has now raised a partition between the sexes such as is found in the aquarium where it becomes necessary to teach the pike to allow the carp, also, to live: every time the pike makes a dash at the carp he strikes his head against the obstruction, until the motive of repression becomes so strong that the glass wall can be taken away and both carp and pike live together in peace.

CHAPTER VI

THE INFLUENCE OF THE WOMAN MOVEMENT UPON MARRIAGE

CERTAIN feminists believe that the woman movement has accomplished such meagre results in regard to the reorganisation of family right for the sole reason that men, who once created the right for their own advantage, still cling to the injustice out of egoism. These feminists forget that the family is the social form of life in which tradition has the greatest power. It speaks here with the voice of the blood; it works through our deepest instincts, our strongest needs of life, our innermost feelings, as these have developed through many thousands of years under the influences which were exercised in and through the family. To accomplish in this sphere not only reforms upon paper but also vigorous modifications—that is, new laws and customs which are rooted in new spiritual conditions of the people as a whole—is more necessary than that man grant women a share in legislation. Innumerable individual human vicissitudes must be experienced and repeated in new forms, entering finally into the universal consciousness, before such spiritual soil can be formed. The man became and remained the head of the family because all experiences and social factors once made this arrangement most advantageous for father, mother, and children. Woman will be able to realise her new ideas in regard to love-life and mother-right to the degree in which she demonstrates, not only in speech and writing but also in vigorous daily living, that these ideals surpass in vital effect those which now obtain.

In the last half century, among the Germanic peoples, however, the family life has already undergone essential transformations, while the Romantic world still continues to exhibit features which in the first half of the 19th century were typical even among these peoples. Marriages are arranged by the father, divorce is considered either a sin or a shame, the paternal power is still absolute, the homogeneous relationship among all the members of the family—in joy and sorrow—is inviolable. The feeling of the son for the mother, bordering almost upon Madonna worship, and the passion of the father for their little children, must, however, always have been more characteristic of the Romance peoples than of the Germans.

Among the latter the attainment of individualism, first in the sphere of legislation, still more in that of customs, most of all in that of mode of thought and feeling, has altered the position of the individual in the family. While the family exhibited fifty years ago a tightly closed unity, in which women had only slight significance, now the wife as well as the husband, mother as well as father, daughter as well as son, assert their personality, not only *in* the family, but often even *against* the family. Wives draw the arguments for their self assertion most frequently from the principles of the woman movement.

Truly, in the course of the century, many married women have succeeded in finding expression for their significant universal human or feminine attributes in marriage, and thus have ennobled it. But the self-conscious effort to elevate the position of the wife began simultaneously with the demand that no human right could be denied to a woman upon the ground of her sex, whether within or without marriage.

Individualism has already made personal love, instead of family interest, decisive for the consummation of a marriage. In the name of her personality as of her work, woman desires with ever greater right full majority and legal equality with man in marriage. Against individualism, the doctrine of evolution now advocates certain limitations of the personal erotic freedom to consummate marriage, but advocates at the same time, contrary to the Christian sexual ethics, new freedom for the sake of the higher development of the race. Here comes into effect, the new conception of life by which the possibilities of development and of happiness in the earthly life have acquired a new value and force.

The ultimate heights of the modern conception of sex-life are indicated by erotic idealism, which since "La Nouvelle Héloise" has by poets and dreamers been continually elevated, while world-renowned lovers showed the possibility of this wonderful love. In addition to all these influences of the spirit of the time upon the transformation of marriage, come the *indirect* effects of the woman movement. Thanks to the vibrations in which this movement has set the "spirit of the time," many an ordinary man now accords to his wife that power and authority in the family which the law still denies her; yes, many commonplace people of both sexes now desire from their marriage things of which their equals fifty years ago did not even dream. If one adds also the decisive influences which the political-economic conditions of the present exercise upon the family life, one has found some of the threads which form the woof of the unalterable warp, a woof which makes the marriage of the present a variegated and unquiet fabric, whose pattern exhibits primeval oriental motives beside those in newest "modern style."

Here it is of the greatest importance to indicate the zigzag line which denotes the alternate repulsion and attraction that under the influence of the woman movement marriage has had for woman.

First came the little crowd of "masculine women" with their hatred of marriage and man.

Then the great working army that forgot, over the human rights of woman, that to these also must belong the right to fulfil her duty as a being of sex, and not alone the right to be "independent of marriage" through her work. Then came the reaction against this incompleteness. At this time, the nature of woman was called an "empty capsule," which received its content only from man: a "cry of the blood," which finds its answer in the child. There was no other "woman question" than the possibility of living erotically a complete life. One woman wished this in love without marriage, another in love without children, a third in children without marriage, a fourth in children without love—"A work and a child" was the life cry—a fifth woman wished the man only for the sake of the child, a sixth the child only for the sake of the man, and the seventh wished both only for her own sake!

The conviction of some women that the common erotic life of man and woman must have also a spiritual life-value for two human souls, filling out and developing each other, was called "Ibsenism." And after the ideal demands which Ibsen pressed upon the consciousness of the time, many men—and not a few women—found relaxation after their spiritual over-exertion, if they desired nothing more from one another than "the sound happiness of the senses." Woman's "personality," "equality," and "human right" were old playthings, relegated to the rubbish heap.

The reaction against this reaction is now in progress. Just now—and equally one-sided as will be shown later—woman's universal humanity is emphasised at the expense of the instinct life; her social labour-duty, at the expense of the domestic life; her personality, at the expense of the family.

Among all these zigzag movements, more deeply thoughtful women continually sought to recall that neither the universal human nor the sexual being of woman must be over-developed at the expense of the other qualities of her being; that perfect humanity signifies for neither sex that the spiritual life has suppressed the sex-life or sex, the soul-life, but that both find in a third higher condition their full redemption and harmony. Through great love, exceptional natures already create this condition; but what to-day only exceptional natures attain, culture can gradually make attainable for many.

This great love demands fidelity. But often only one—ordinarily the woman—experiences this great feeling. And then not even the deepest devotion on her part suffices to preserve the community of life. To preserve the form for the purpose of guarding the inner emptiness, as was done earlier, is repugnant to the erotic consciousness of the modern woman. This is the deepest reason why the modern woman—even also the modern developed man—becomes continually more undecided about contracting marriage. They both know that the passion which attracts two beings is not synonymous with a sympathy which arises through the harmony of their natures, which must not be so complete that nothing remains of the unexpected and mysterious that is so essential an element of love. The modern woman asks herself, "What can prove to me that an erotic sympathy is profound, real, decreed by nature, life-long?" And she asks with good reason. If two lovers who know that they make each other happy with all the senses, constrained themselves, each in a corner of a room fettered to a stool, blindfolded, to entertain each other three hours daily for three months, this test would probably prevent a great number of marriages void of sympathy. But it would furnish no guaranty that those who consummated the marriage after such a concentrated soul interchange, would hold out. For souls which in a certain stage of development seem inexhaustible can be so transformed that they experience only satiety for each other. The young wife of to-day is deeply conscious of what a new problem for each newly married woman marriage is. She knows how impossible it is to foresee what difficulties will be encountered and whether good intentions and tactful adaptation will succeed in overcoming these difficulties. She knows that, even if the written law made her wholly equal to man, even if she made herself that equal by entering only into a marriage of the higher, newer conscience, yet all the inner, most difficult, deepest problems still remain. This certainly induces many women to become only the beloved, the mistress, of the man who wishes no community of life, but only happy hours. Many more women still strike the possibilities of erotic happiness out of their plan of life, because they have not experienced the ideal love of which they dreamed, or else could not realise it.[1]

[1] This idealism has naturally part also in the fact that, for example, two thirds of the women who have gone through college in America do not marry, and find in club life a compensation for domestic life. But other motives also must often play a part here, from the desire to devote herself entirely to one of the lifeworks serviceable to mankind, to the egoism of spiritually barren young girls with its distaste for burdens and restraint.

A keen-sighted observer who recently spent a half year in North America corroborated what many have already stated: that the student and working young American girls devote themselves with true passion to the cultivation of their beauty, their toilette, their flirtations. All this belongs for her to the "Fine Arts" and as such is an end sufficient in itself, while for European women these arts, as a rule, are still means for alluring men to marriage. While study or work often makes European women in outer sense less "womanly," although her soul always guards its full power to love, in America the reverse is the case: the outer appearance is bewitchingly womanly, but the soul no longer vibrates for love. The sexual sterility which Maudsley already prophesied thirty years ago, when he spoke about the "sexless ants," has been partly realised, partly chosen voluntarily. In Europe it still frequently happens that a young woman who has put love aside for the sake of study or work is suddenly seized by an irresistible passion; in America, on the contrary, this is extremely rare. Women students look down upon the less cultured men, who ordinarily finish their studies earlier in order to earn a livelihood. The sympathy which they need, women find more easily in their own sex. The unmarried have quite

Sometimes their doubt, in regard to the duration of love and the unity of souls, decides them, another time the longing for a personal life-work is the reason for their determination—a life-work for which these women have suffered so keenly, been deprived of so much, and have so struggled, that it has become passionately dear to them, and they feel that a complete renunciation of the erotic life is easier than the torment of being "drawn and quartered," as the death penalty of the Middle Ages was called—a quartering between profession, husband, home, and children. And the result

---

the same social position as the married and do not desire children. If they finally marry, it is ordinarily because a more brilliant position is offered them than the one which they could create themselves, and the man is then considered and treated as a money-getter.

My authority emphasises also that the young students or working girls are ordinarily less original, of less personal significance, less individually developed, than the older women, especially women's rights women, who often have not studied but have grown grey in marriage and motherhood, in self-development and in social work. The interesting significant American feminists were women between the ages of fifty and ninety; the woman of the present generation, however, which now enjoys the fruits of the work of the older generation, is, in spite of excellent scholarship and great working proficiency, less a woman and less a human being, less a personality.

These wholly fresh observations, which were communicated to me during the printing of my book, seem to me to confirm so strongly my point of view that I wish to repeat them here.

But in France and elsewhere mothers tell us how clear, intelligent, and universally interested their daughters are, and at the same time how critical, how free from ardour and enthusiasm. It is not the hasty love-marriage that many mothers now fear for their daughters, but a worldly-wise marriage without love.

usually demonstrates that celibacy is wiser than the compromise. It is most frequently the case, —in Europe at least,—if the work of the unmarried woman had no personal character, and if the home is not dependent upon the earnings of the wife, that she gives up her professional work after her marriage.

Against this sacrifice, however, the higher erotic idealism has begun to rebel and has, thereby, come into conflict with the conservative direction of feminism, which while planning to make the wife equal to the husband, adheres firmly to the present marriage as protection for wife and children.

It is this point of view that is condemned by the new idealism. For it "protection" signifies, in its innermost meaning, that the man buys love and the woman sells it, which is considered "moral," while it is considered immoral for a man to sell love and for a woman to buy it. The "protection" in this relationship has as result that the "virtue" of the maid is synonymous with untouched sexual nature, and that of the wife, with physical fidelity; while the "virtue" of the youth and the man is judged from an entirely different point of view.

The relationship affording "protection" has also brought with it the idea that a woman could not show her love as openly as a man, except when he was proud and poor and she was rich. Only when the duty of support on the part of the man ceases, will woman be able to demand the same chastity and fidelity from him as he demands from her; she will then be able, quite as proudly and naturally as he, to show the flowering of her being—her love—instead of as now increasing her demand in the marriage market by artful dissimulation. As long as maintenance, within or outside of marriage, is the price for "possession" of the woman, the man will consider the woman as "his," and the more submissive she is the more fully she satisfies his feeling of ownership. Now marriage has become only an affair of custom, a common death or comatose condition, because neither party needs trouble himself to keep the love of the other. Only when woman, through her work, can lead an existence worthy of a human being, when no woman will sell her love but every woman can freely give it, will man experience what perfect womanly devotion is. And when no man can "possess" love but must remain worthy of love in order to be loved then only will women, on their side, experience what tenderness and fine feeling masculine devotion can attain.

This, the purest and warmest erotic idealism, is the morality of the future. But the way to its realisation is not, as many women believe to-day, that mothers, even, should continue their work of earning a livelihood, but that way whose direction I have elsewhere pointed out.[1]

[1] See *Love and Ethics*, Ralph Fletcher Seymour, Chicago, and also *Mutter und Kind*, published in Germany only, Pan-Verlag. My plan is a paternity assessment upon society as a contribution

Here we have to do, however, only with the spiritual conditions which arise in the marriage of to-day, whether the wife has retained her work or has given it up.

Even the cultivated modern man, who brings

to the maintenance of children and a compensation of motherhood by the state.

Society has already shown by a series of institutions, maternity assurance, infants' milk distribution, clothing and feeding of children, and many kindred social efforts, that the maintenance afforded by the father is not sufficient for the young generation; quite as little is the mother's care, which is supplemented by other means, crèches, etc. But when the *child* finally becomes the unconscious "head of the family," then it will be the affair of society to requite maternity. Marriage will then signify only the living together of two people upon the ground of love and the common parenthood of children. *Maternal right* will *in law* take the place of *paternal right*, but *in reality* the father will continue to retain all the influence upon the children which he *personally* is able to exert, just as has been hitherto the case with the mother.

In such circumstances there will be no more illegitimate children; no mothers driven out from the care of tender children to earn their daily bread; no fathers who avoid their economic duties toward their children, and who cannot be compelled by society to perform at least that paternal duty which animals perform now better than men: that of contributing their part to the maintenance of their progeny. There will be no mothers who for the sake of their own and their children's maintenance need to stay with a brutal man; no mothers who, in case of a separation, can be deprived of their children on any ground except that of their own unworthiness. In a word, society must—upon a higher plane—restore the arrangement which is already found in the lower stages of civilisation, the arrangement which nature herself created: that mother and child are most closely bound together, that they together, above all, form the family, in which the father enters through the mother's or his own free will.

to the human personality of his wife admiration and sympathy, seeks in her always that "womanliness" to which Goethe has given the classic expression: the finely reserved, quiet, strong, self-contained woman, reposing harmoniously in the fulness of her own nature, a maternally lovely being, wholly "natural," a "beautiful soul," observing, creative, but using these gifts only to create a home. These creative offices the modern man who loves desires to assure, when he wishes to "maintain" his wife, and begs her to abandon the outside commercial work in which he foresees a danger to the beautiful life together of which both dream. The woman who along with her new self-conscious individuality and her profound culture has guarded the "old" devotion, understands ordinarily this desire of the man. She chooses, in spite of her idealism, as he wishes, in cases where her work has not been very personal. If she has worked in the same field as the man, then she converts her gifts into comprehension of him, into personal interest for all his interests; and these marriages in which the wife has enjoyed the same education as the man, but later has devoted herself entirely to the home, are, as a rule, the happiest marriages of the present time. But in the proportion in which her work was creative, is the difficulty of the choice. In the case where the productive power has the strength of genius, the modern man will scarcely utter such a wish and in those circumstances the modern woman will not grant it And because the woman of genius is generally a complete human being, with strong erotic as well as universal human demands, she chooses often compromise. She finds in love, in motherhood, new revelations; and in the mysterious depths of her nature, the productive element of the maternal function has an elevating influence upon her gift of creative power. Thus the energy temporarily diminished by motherhood is restored. And her uneasy conscience, because she must entrust to others much of the care and education of the children, is appeased by the consciousness that she has often given to mankind richer natures, and so more significant children, than more devoted mothers, and that her own nature, because of the double creative activity, has attained a ripeness and richness which make her personality more significant for husband and children than if she had given up her calling to please them. These thoughts cannot, however, prevent the daily conflict between her feelings of love and the impossibility, in times of strong spiritual production, of giving expression to it. The very proximity of the children consumes at such times too much nervous energy. And since all creation requires selfishness—in the sense of concentration upon one's *own needs* in order to be able to work creatively and to sink oneself in the work—while all love's solicitude requires active *attention* to the *needs of the loved ones*, the conflict must remain permanent and *insoluble*.

In this conviction, many women of genius choose the lesser conflict: marriage without children. Such a relationship occurs not infrequently in our time in this way: a man of feeling through the work of a woman is first moved by her being. The man is in that case often the younger or the less developed. At first, marriage brings both a rich happiness. But later comes a time when the power of the personality of the woman of genius becomes too strong for the man; when he feels himself exhausted by all the sensitiveness and impatience which charge the air about a creative personality with electricity. He has now had enough of the rich spiritual exchange and longs for a woman who is only fresh richness, sunny quiet, easy docility; the now vanished "ingénue" would be the type of woman who most of all could entrance him.

In another case, it is the wife who becomes wearied, when the man can no longer keep pace with her development nor afford her new inspiration. The erotic life of the woman as well as of the man of genius exhibits two phases: in one they are attracted by their opposite, in the other by a congeniality of souls; in one phase they have sought sentiment, intimacy, nature; in the other, soul, passion, culture. The order changes in different cases, but the phenomenon repeats itself. What both consciously or unconsciously desire of love is not another individuality to love but only a means of inspiration.

Yet one thing may be emphasised: the richer the nature of a woman is and the greater her talents, the more life-determining love will be for her; at one time making her existence desolate, at another time making it fruitful. For the woman of genius is less able than the man to renounce her own fate. This the man is capable of doing, in the midst of passion, without his work suffering thereby in vigour and strength; the woman on the contrary —even the genius—loses more easily her creative impulse in happiness, her creative power in unhappiness.

In this connection it may be recalled that many of the most gifted, most highly developed woman personalities of to-day have produced nothing, but have been what a Frenchman has called "les grandes inspiratrices." These have not, indeed, like the "Ladies" of the Middle Ages, been worshipped at a distance by knights and poets; but they have had an influence similar to that of Beatrice, through the power of communication of their rich personality in a relationship which had now the character of an "amitié amoureuse," now that of a love imbued with sympathy, which in some cases, infrequently however, led to marriage. I need only mention the name Richard Wagner for the forms of two such women to appear, one of whom, who was his wife, surpassed in personal greatness all independently creative women of her time. But there have always been less unusual women who had significance as propagandists of the ideas of a great man through their specifically feminine gifts of convincing, of diffusing ideas, of modifying views, etc. If the future, because of the wife's zeal for production on her own part, should lose this element of culture, it would be deplorable.

One of the favourite arguments of the woman movement has been that two married people working in the same profession had the best opportunities for understanding each other and consequently also for being happy. And truly they can best talk shop with each other. But that is what the working man needs least of all in his home; there he seeks rather relaxation from his calling, or at least a quite disinterested, immediate sympathy with its annoyances or joys. When one of the married fellow workmen needs exactly this sympathy, the other is perhaps busy or too tired to be capable of such lively interest as the other expects. Or one has experienced disappointments, the other joys, and then a real sympathy is still more difficult. To these crossings of mood is added also the unintentional, involuntary competition, which the similarity of vocation brings with it. The wife gains patients, the husband does not; his picture is praised, hers is pulled to pieces; she comes home from the theatre victorious, he after a defeat. During work, the criticism of one often disturbs the other; after the work, the criticism of the press disturbs the harmony of both. Love wishes to fuse them into one being, the outer world compels them always to feel themselves separate. In the beginning they think: "Nothing can come between us." But if both do not possess a rare tenderness as well as rare fineness of soul, soon needles of ice fly through the air between them. Only when the wife, as is the case so often in France, puts her ability into her husband's affairs does this common interest prevent rivalry.

Whether the province of the husband and wife is the same or not, difficulty always results from the wife's commercial or professional work in that she rarely finds a good substitute for the domestic and maternal duties. And when the husband sees the house badly managed and the children ill-bred, he tries according to his strength to render assistance or, as more frequently happens, seeks his comfort outside the home. But even if these stumbling-blocks may be cleared away by other feminine hands, the fact still remains that the wife because of her work must demand sacrifices on the part of the man such as his work has required at all times from the wife. She is often compelled to forego much of the society of her husband, of his solicitude and tenderness because he has no available time. Now each of the married people has consideration for the leisure of the other and for all other severe conditions of the work. But beside these favourable results stands also the detrimental fact that each suppresses his claims upon the sympathy of the other, as well as the wish to express his own, whenever this receiving and giving would interfere with the work. If this has become for one or for both a real passion, then the passion blinds him to everything that does not concern the work, and causes alternately joy or suffering. Each of the married couple then disturbs the other by moods, and each needs to be cherished by the other. The tenderness which neither can give to the other, they find perhaps in a third.

But in those cases where the work is not passionately absorbing or where both husband and wife are persons of understanding, rather than of feeling, marriages of colleagues turn out well. Each has in the other an intelligent, appreciative friend; the common work together is rich, and neither gives nor requires more than the other is able to reciprocate. The education of the wife makes her a good organiser in the home, which is comfortable without the work's suffering thereby. When this is not too strenuous for either, but after the close of a reasonable working time, the two meet spiritually free in the home, the duties of which they often share—then the domestic life is happy and the work progresses easily, as long as there are no children. When children arrive, then there begins for the wife, even in such marriages, a life beyond her strength.

But since nature, in the interest of the race, often makes opposites attractive to each other, one may find a husband, full of feeling, who loves children, united to a wife for whom science is the greatest value of life, while she relegates feeling to a lower plane and considers motherhood an animal function. In place of the tenderness and of the children for which the husband longed, he has to participate in the victories and defeats of a woman of science. Or we see a wife who dreamed of an intimate life with her husband and who sacrificed her work to it; but the life together was wrecked upon the husband's artist concentration, and the wife had to suffer under a twofold emptiness: the lack of her work and the lack of happiness. Then one sees instances where the wife retained her work because it was economically necessary and because she hoped out of the richness of her young strength to be able to fulfil all duties. And all this she was able to do except one thing—to preserve under the excessive strain her beauty, her power of charm, the elasticity of her nature. Perhaps she belonged to the very highest among the new women who are so undivided, so proud, who think so highly of themselves, of man, of love, that they are beyond a wholly justified coquetry and rest blindly upon the uniting power of spiritual congeniality. But the day comes perhaps when these strong and, in all other respects, wise women have nothing other than freedom to give to the man whose senses, whose fancy, need that charm which the wife no longer possesses. In case, however, the man's nature is not of those for whom the silken threads of daily domestic comfort form the strong band, but on the contrary is of the sort which needs renewal, then the very absence of the wife, occasioned temporarily by the work, can keep the relationship long fresh. This is upon the assumption that she understands what some of these women do not understand: to give, but in such a way that the man always longs for more; to remain sweetheart, not only friend; to be able to jest, not only to talk seriously. The modern wife of to-day, tested upon so many subjects, is often deeply mistaken in regard to the *kind* of "ministry" the man needs. The simple wisdom of their grandmothers consisted in this: to give much and to require nothing, always to subordinate themselves to the man with gentleness and humility, never to assert themselves before him as a free, self-determining personality. The wives of to-day, sacredly convinced of the right and freedom of women, succeed better in asserting their personality than in pleasing their husbands, and the quantity of their demands is often more noteworthy than the quality of their gifts. That many modern marriages turn out well shows that the adaptability of the modern husband is beginning to be even as great as that of the wife in former times!

The marriage is absolutely wrecked when the wife brings to it all the new demands of woman, but the husband all the primeval instincts of his sex. What in each sex relationship most intimately unites or most deeply sunders is and remains the erotic depth of nature in each. And the difference in this respect between the men and women of the present ever more widely separates them, and this division becomes fatal to innumerable individual lovers of to-day, as well as for the attitude of the sexes toward marriage in general. The erotically symmetrical woman views with hostility the dualism in the erotic nature of the modern man. This dualism evinces itself, with innumerable nuances it is true, in three typical ways: infinite erotic discussion, but inability to be stirred by it either with the soul or with the senses; ability to love only with the senses, not with the soul; and finally looking down upon the senses and desiring "spiritual love" only. For the modern completely developed woman the chattering vacuity, the animal instinct, the ascetic spirituality, are equally repellent. And yet it happens that the rosy mist of love can bring such a woman to a point where she creates for herself an illusion out of one of the above mentioned types. Most frequently this occurs in the case of the vigorous man who divines nothing of the spiritual content of the woman whose outer appearance has charmed him. The tragedy of the modern woman is then like that which Hebbel has revealed in *Judith*, that the sex being in her is attracted by the muscular masculinity, which her human personality hates as her mortal enemy. For as a personality she admires in man only the spiritual strength of the man. The man on his part regrets his mistake that he did not choose a pretty amiable girl "of the old sort," who would punctually lay his table and willingly share his bed; a woman "into whose head Ibsen had put no fancies," who "had not allowed herself to be talked into some folly by feminism."

Among such "follies," similar men, and many others as well, include the demand advanced by the woman movement for the married woman's property right, as well as a specified income for the wife working in the home, who however has to contribute from her property or her "remuneration" as housekeeper to the common household —a corollary which is always forgotten by the antifeminist writers who assert that "the man becomes a slave when he has to work for the whole, but the wife may retain everything of hers." (*Strindberg.*)

The modern woman who before her marriage was independent, owing to her work, abhors the thought of a request for money—this most painful moment even in the happiest marriages—to so great a degree that this aversion determines the wife in some cases to keep up her own work. If on the contrary she has given this up, the consciousness of her earlier independence makes her often so sensitive that she feels herself injured by a protest however delicate in regard to the expenditure of money. More than one man has regretted, in consequence of the unreasonable demands of his wife, that he ever begged her to give up her own work. There are women, on the other hand, who continue their work and thereby only increase the incapability of a good-for-nothing man. In such cases, it avails little that in many countries the law now allows the wife free disposal of the income from her labour. Notwithstanding this, the assertion is ridiculous that "if the man drinks up the money of his wife it is with her consent," and "it is therefore of no avail to alter the law." For it makes a significant difference in the relative position of the man and wife whether the law gives him the *right* to it, or whether he takes it by force. But in this as in other cases, the woman movement obviously cannot free women so long as they are impelled by unconscious forces from within to actions and sacrifices at variance with their conscious personality. The one thing which the woman movement has already achieved and can continue to achieve, is that the undue encroachment of the men ceases to have legal protection.

It is undeniable, on the other hand, that the unmarried woman's personal and economic independence fashions wives who in marriage show themselves in a high degree egotistic, but who yet incessantly scold about man's egotism, wives who themselves exhibit very little devotion and fine feeling, but place very great importance upon consideration. These wives were the ones whom fifty years ago men called "graters." But the lack of amiability, which in certain women was usually due to childbirth, has nevertheless in modern woman, at least during the freedom of her girlhood, been unrestrained habit. Her firm —and just—decision not to be "subservient" to her husband has resulted in, first, an armed peace, later, a war, in which the wife's work is one of the projectiles. "I have my work, why should I stay here to be used up and tormented?" she asks herself. And when such questions begin, there is usually but one answer.

There is one decided advantage in giving to the woman the opportunity to earn her living: she has again acquired thereby significance in the home, while the generation of women, who neither co-operated *productively* in the home nor assumed all the duties of the mother, were regarded by man with less respect than, on the one side, their grandmothers who *produced* all of the household requisites, on the other side, their now independent self-supporting granddaughters. Only when society *recompenses the vocation of mother*, can woman find in this a full equivalent for self-supporting labour.

Another typical group of our time is formed by the numerous women for whom no choice remains in regard to their work, since it is of a kind that they must give up because of the removal to another place, or more frequently because they find so much work in the new home that every thought of anything further outside must cease. Those who think that industry has made the work of the wife in the home to-day superfluous, speak only of the *great cities*, and usually only of *opulent families in the great cities*, where they are in a position to buy cheaper everything that the labour of the wife could produce. But in the country, among all classes, the mother must be the director of the work; and in all country homes in moderate circumstances—as in countless poor or not very well-to-do city families—the work of the mother is still frequently indispensable, and in addition is more economical than her earnings out of the house could be, especially since the developed modern woman is usually capable of a more rational housekeeping than the woman of earlier times.

But while the mothers of that time knew nothing except housework, those of to-day have often, as unmarried and self-supporting women, enjoyed a freedom of movement and opportunities of development which, now that they are over-burdened with household cares, they may seriously miss. The work of the mother is now still further increased by the difficulty of getting servants—at least capable ones—and also by the demands of luxury. The result of this again is that hospitality in the home decreases, that the watchword of the time, "the windows of the house wide open to the world, fresh air in the home, no creeping into the chimney corner," is so interpreted that warmth and intimacy vanish. Yes, the overworked mother often herself insists that the family leave the house and seek some place of recreation for the annual festivals, which were once the children's happiest and brightest recollections of home.

The fact that most modern women of culture devote themselves to some branch of social work, often to several, contributes still further to the over-exertion of the mother. Even when this occurs from pure altruism, the motive cannot prevent such altruism from becoming sometimes a disease of which one may die quite as surely as of other diseases. This death is quite as immoral as any other resulting from neglected hygiene. No one has the right to perish from altruism, except when destruction is the *condition* of his fulfilling his duty. But in many cases the occasion is the widely ramified social activity of the woman for whom the home now often falls short; not a result of altruism, but a manifestation of that desire for power which once was satisfied in the family. Or it may be a form of the hysteria characteristic of the present time. In the sixteenth century, the hysterical were burned as witches; now they "sacrifice" themselves to an activity which offers them in reality the variety, the intoxication of publicity —in a word, the life stimulus they need. But even sound, sincere, and conscientious women are driven by the woman movement and by social work to assume pseudo duties, for which the real duties are pushed aside. If instead of instituting official inquiries among wives and mothers as to what they can accomplish, one should direct the same questions to their husbands and children, these would, if they dared be honest, testify that *they* must pay the price for the altruistic activity.

Since the work of married women outside the home, the woman movement, and the social work began, one seldom finds a wholly sound, joyous, harmonious wife and mother. The constant complaint of the modern woman is that she "never has time." The minority who live a life of luxury, wholly free from work, while the husband works feverishly to provide the luxury which neither will forego, telephone away a quarter of the day making appointments concerning the toilette, visits, and amusements, which take up the remaining three quarters of the day. And others, loaded down with household work or divided between this and work for their livelihood, how shall they find time!

Least of all have they the time necessary for the countless little tokens of tenderness which intensify all relationships between people. A French mother who became a widow and brought up her children by means of her own work received from her son, grown to a youth, the judgment: "Thou hast never loved us." Too late, it became clear to her that "it requires time to love," that it is not enough to feel love, and, looked at as a whole, to act with love—no, love must be expressed. And for this the harassed mother of to-day lacks time and quiet.

Formerly, it was only the husband and father who had no time; the wife and mother had it and could thus preserve the warmth of the home. But now?

There are now, it is true, many women with so few claims that they think they have fulfilled the fourfold task. In reality, they have fulfilled all their duties imperfectly, or eliminated one task for a time in order to be able to accomplish the others. *No woman has ever been at the same time all* that a wife can be to her husband, a mother to her children, a housewife to her house, a working woman to her work. In the last capacity the difficulty of the married woman is still further increased by the present competition, as also by the fact that the better a person works the more work falls to her, so that an exact and reasonable division of time between work and home is often rendered quite impossible.

In addition to all these difficulties arising through actualities, there are finally also those evoked by the "spirit of the time." A wife has, for example, decided to give up a vocation which she saw was not compatible with her home. But she stills finds no rest. She is harassed by the demand of the "spirit of the time" that a married woman should be able to take care of the house as well as to accomplish outside personal work. The husband, also influenced by the "spirit of the time," thinks the same or feels painfully the fact that his wife, for love of him, has sacrificed the exercise of a talent, in which he perhaps has felt a personal interest; the longing for the vocation awakens in her, and she resumes her work, with the result that, if she has energetically resisted the lassitude that comes with beginning motherhood, she and the child must suffer later. Or she lives in a permanent state of over-exertion which finally culminates in nervous conditions under which the whole family must share her suffering. Had she been able to follow in peace her instinct to strike deep root in the home soil and to enlarge and enrich her being by the annual growth of ring after ring of her production of love, then the essential values would have been increased for all. Now, she is led astray by a biased opinion of the time, which owes its effectiveness to the single fact that the opinionated resolutely turn their back upon all facts.

Thanks to these ideas of the time propagated by certain feminists, we see increasing numbers of women who perform their "social duty" as the telegraph poles perform their function; while such duty could have been fulfilled as the tree grows in a garden: blooming, fruit-bearing, joyful, joy-bringing.

CHAPTER VII

THE INFLUENCE OF THE WOMAN MOVEMENT UPON MOTHERHOOD

BECAUSE it has increased the culture of woman and her feeling of personal responsibility, the woman movement has had its influence, both directly and indirectly, upon the postponement of the legal and customary marriage age. Since young girls have exercised their brains as much as the boys have, they are no longer so far in advance of the boys in physical development. But when modern girls finish their studies they are physically as well as psychically more universally developed than their grandmothers were. They know much more of the difficulties and realities of life, not least of the sexual life. And this knowledge has instilled in them a reluctance to undertake too early the serious and difficult task of motherhood. They have greater need of truth and culture, and less tendency to erotic visionary dreaming than girls of their age in the middle of the previous century; their desire for work and their social feeling fix goals, and they work with all their might to attain them. And because, as already explained, both sexes have for each other a more many-sided attraction than the merely erotic, young people are more careful, more choice, in their erotic decisions. The finest young girls of to-day are penetrated by the Nietzschean idea, that marriage is the combined will of two people to create a new being greater than themselves. But their joy does *not* consist in the fact "that the man wills"; they are themselves "will," and above all they have the will to choose the right father for their children, not only for their own sake but for the sake of the children.

If it be true that immediate, "blind," erotic attraction is most instinctively correct in choice, then the present comrade life of young people and the increased clear-sightedness which it gives, as well as the increasing erotic idealism of young girls, are not unconditionally advantageous to the new race. The question is, however, still undecided. Here it may only be emphasised that the young girl of to-day, in spite of all intellectual development, is still won always by powerful spiritual-sensual love, which the woman movement has too long considered as a negligible quantity. Under the influence of the doctrine of evolution, young girls begin to understand that their value as members of society depends essentially upon their value for the propagation of mankind; all the more they realise the duty of physical culture which will enable them to fulfil this function better; they no longer consider their erotic longing as impure and ugly but as pure and beautiful. It is out of this soul condition that the different movements for the protection of mothers and children, theoretically considered, have proceeded. These are at present the most important "woman movements," although unrecognised by the older woman movement. And this older movement has not yet recognised the fact that, because of present marriage conditions, the degenerate, uneducated, decrepit, have greater opportunity for propagating the race, both within and outside of marriage, than the young, sound, pure-minded, and loving; that it can therefore *be no sin*, from the point of view of the race, if the latter become parents without marriage, nor should it be a subject of shame from the social point of view. All women's rights have little value, until this one thing is attained: that a woman who through her illegitimate motherhood has lost nothing of her personal worth, but on the contrary has proved it, does not forfeit social esteem.

Our time can point to women who have been typical of the reform tendencies of the century in this respect. Some of these women, if they really accomplished the unprecedented task of "a child and a work," have drawn their strength for the task out of precisely the commonplace, homely qualities and sterling virtues, contrary to which they believed they were acting when they became mothers, driven by a power greater than their *conscious* personality. Others again became mothers with the consent of their whole personality. They were clear that they thus made use of the masculine rights and freedom which feminism first brought home to women. And although many advocates of women's rights refrain from such consequences of their ideas, the women who in other respects determine their conduct of life by their own free personal choice recognise that this, their *real* "emancipation," is a fruit of the woman movement.

In Europe, however, most women under thirty still dare to dream of motherhood in a love marriage as the greatest happiness and the highest duty of life.[1]

But, as direct and indirect result of the woman movement, the fact none the less remains that there is found *among women an increasing dis-*

[1] An inquiry instituted among English women as to whether they would prefer to be men or women gave as a result the fact that, out of about 7000 who answered, two-thirds wished to remain women and this above all in order to be mothers, while a third wished to be men. This indicated probably the highest figure of the disinclination for maternity which such a *European* inquiry could elicit. But even these women who wish to marry and to become mothers feel the pressure of the idea created by the zealots of the woman movement which finds expression often in the following conversation between two former schoolmates about a third: "And A—— what is she doing now?"—"Nothing—she is married and has children."

The old folk legend about the girl who trampled on the bread she was carrying to her mother because she wished to go dry-shod, can serve as symbol of many modern women zealots: life's great, sound values are offered for the meal; vanity sits down alone to partake of them.

inclination for maternity, a reluctance which deprives mankind of many superior mothers, while at the same time woman's commercial work for self-support in all classes increases her sterility or makes her incapable of the suckling so vitally important for the children.

That the modern woman, because of individual fate or her own choice, often remains unmarried is no danger in and for itself. This fact, as I have emphasised above, is connected with a number of cultural and material conditions, which sometime will be altered, and then woman's desire for marriage will again increase. The real danger has appeared only since women have begun to strengthen the tendency to celibacy by the amaternal theory, which now confuses the feminine brain and leads the feminine instinct astray.

The woman movement in and with this influence upon maternity sinks to the lowest point of the scale according to the criterion of worth employed here: the elevation of the life of the individual and of the race. In this we stand in our time before a twofold mystery, which lies in the circumstance that not only women—women "with breasts made right to suckle babes"—emphasise this stultifying influence, but that there are men, each the son of a mother, who also propagate it. These men have allowed themselves to be blinded by the false logic concerning women, which declares that since rich mothers do not wish to fulfil the duties of a mother and the poor cannot fulfil them, superior social organisations must be created for that purpose; in other words, instigated by a mere temporary unpleasant discrepancy, we will create a new, a different order of things. But, if this obtained universally, it would inflict incomparably greater injury upon mankind than do present unhappy conditions.

Upon the whole, however, it is precisely as a result of this tendency that the deepest hostility of men against feminism has developed. The fact that the idea of evolution is now beginning to enter into the flesh and blood of man also contributes its share to this feeling. Just as formerly a man wished heirs for his personal and real estate and for his name, he now desires inheritors of his being; he desires an eternal life, which becomes a certainty only by means of parenthood, whereby the individual as father or mother lives on physically and spiritually, in body and soul, in his children and grandchildren down to the last of his descendants. This conception has made the sex instinct again holy, as it was for the pagans. This new reverence for their duty as beings of sex now induces many young men to guard their sexual health and strength by an asceticism the motive of which is the exact opposite of that which determined the asceticism called forth by Christianity, the asceticism which was fear of the sex instinct as impure and as a temptation to sin. Now the innermost aim of young men's creative desire is the higher development of mankind. Love becomes for them the condition by which they can most perfectly redeem their religious certainty of being part of a great design, their religious longing for harmony with life's creative desire, with the infinite.

There are now men who work most zealously for the ennoblement of the race—"eugenics," as this effort is called in England—as well as for the protection of mother and child—"puericulture," as this endeavour is called in France. There are men who write excellent works upon the psychology of the child, and upon sexual instruction; men, who, in art and poetry, give expression to the new veneration for the sanctity of generation, for motherhood, for the child. The finest thing written about the child as a cultural power is written by an American.[1] Painting has now new devotional pictures of the Mother with her Child, especially those conceived by a Frenchman and an Italian.[2] The most beautiful representation of youth's new desire for love is by a German sculptor. Likewise a German, Nietzsche, has the most profound conception of parenthood and education as the means whereby humanity will cross over the bridge of the men of to-day to the superman.

Only when all this is realised can one conceive what the feelings of these new men must be when they meet those new women "who are no longer

---

[1] Bret Harte, *The Luck of Roaring Camp.*
[2] E. Carrière and Segantini.   [3] Max Kruse, *Liebesgruppe.*

willing to be slaves of the instinct for the propagation of the race"; who see in motherhood "a loss of time from their work"; "an attack upon their beauty"; an obstacle to the refined conduct of life;—a conduct of life certain to debase woman's worth as a child-bearing being, but to elevate her to that exquisite, perfect product of culture, a "woman of the world"; an obstacle also for woman as creator of other objective cultural values. If a man with a father's desires finds himself united with such a woman, he finds himself in marriage quite as much a prostitute as innumerable wives have felt themselves to be when they were mere tools of a man's desire. On the contrary the desire for the elevation of mankind on the part of the new woman and the new man, is evinced in the idea that not the quantity but the quality of the children they give to humanity is most significant; that a land of fewer but more perfect men is a higher culture ideal than the principle still always maintained from the point of view of national competition, that the inhabitants of a country must only be numerous however inferior they may be.

To this wholly new evolutionary conception of life the amaternal women oppose the following train of thought which greatly influences the feeling and desire of women to-day[1]:

[1] This amaternal idea is advanced with great ability in some works of Charlotte Perkins Stetson and Rosa Mayreder. The word amaternal coined by me is used to characterise the theory

Its Influence upon Motherhood 177

Culture now sets new duties for woman, more significant than exclusively natural ones. The more the individual life increases in value, the more the interest for the mere functions of sex declines, and with it also the value of woman *as woman* for a society where, because of motherhood, she has become a being of secondary rank. It evinces lack of ideality if one censures this tendency of the modern woman to renounce maternity for the sake of more spiritual interests. While the mother concentrates herself upon her own child only, the woman who renounces motherhood can extend her being to embrace children as children in general. As a mother, woman is only a being of nature. But the personality, with its multiplicity of feelings and endeavours, demands an independent activity as well as maternity.

To put her entire personality into the education of her children is a twofold error. First and foremost, most mothers are *bad* educators and serve their children better if they entrust them to a born teacher; in the second place, *gifted* children educate

---

subsequently advanced, because the word unmaternal (unmotherly) signifies a *spiritual condition*, the antithesis to "motherliness." The maternal as opposed to the amaternal theory is this: that a woman's life is lived most intensively and most extensively, most individually and most socially; she is for her own part most free, and for others most fruitful, most egoistic and most altruistic, most receptive and most generous, in and with the *physical and psychic exercise of the function of maternity, because of the conscious desire, by means of this function, to uplift the life of the race as well as her own life.*

themselves best and should be spared all educational arts. The mediocre child, who is more susceptible to education, has ordinarily also only mediocre parents, who likewise benefit the children most if they put them in the care of excellent teachers. Children who are *below* mediocrity can also be best educated by specialists. So there remains for the mother, after the first years' care and training, no especial task as educator, at least none in which she can really put her personality. To talk to a mother about the possibilities of a richer office of mother, as educator of her children, she calls lulling her into an illusion under which she must labour only to suffer. A woman who can exercise her personality in another way should not therefore put it into the education of her children.

The amaternal advocates deny that motherliness is the criterion of womanliness; they find this criterion in the form, the external being of woman, in her manner and physical appearance—in a word, in the *outer* expression of the inner disposition, which they deny as typical of womanliness! "Womanliness" is thus reduced to an "æsthetic principle," while woman's spiritual attributes are considered as "universally human"; and the right is granted to the feminine sex to emancipate herself from the result of the heresy that *motherliness* should be the ethical norm for the "being" or "essence" of womanhood. The suitability of woman's *psychic* constitution for her work as mother is not acknowledged as proof that motherliness is the distinguishing characteristic of womanliness. For this constitution is less conspicuous in the higher stages of differentiation. Its suitability was then a phenomenon of adaptation and changed with the conditions of life. Thus this constitution cannot be cited as a reason for limiting woman's personal exercise of her powers. Motherliness is no social instinct. How can motherliness, which we have in common with beasts and savages, be considered as higher than, for example, justice, truth, and other gradually won spiritual values, which woman can promote by her personal activity? The higher the forms of life woman attains, the less will her personality be determined by motherliness. Why then should women bring to the domestic life the sacrifice of their personality, while no one demands this of men? Why shall not woman, just as man, satisfy her demands as a sex-being in marriage and, as for the rest, follow her profession, attend to her spiritual development, her social tasks? Why condemn woman to remain a half-being—that is, with unexercised brain—only because certain of her instincts attract her to man, while he is not constrained to suppress his personality because he in like manner felt himself attracted to woman? It is the old superstition of the family life as "woman's sphere," which still confuses the conception. By the present form of family life woman is "oversexed." Her higher development, as well as that of her husband and children, will be promoted if woman guards her independence by earning her own living, in commercial work conducted beyond the portal of the home; if housekeeping becomes co-operative; if the education of the children is carried on outside the home, in which now the motherly tenderness emasculates the children and fosters in them family sentiment of an egoistic nature and not social feelings. Thus are solved the difficulties which are entailed when the wife's work is carried on outside the home; equipoise between her intellectual and emotional, her sexual and social nature follows, and her worth, as that of a man, will be measured by her human personality, not by her womanliness, her efficacy in the family, for the exercise of which she is now constrained to renounce her personality.

So runs in brief the programme of the amaternals.

.   .   .   .

It has already been indicated that the woman movement, in its *inception*, could gather strength only by combating with all its power the prejudice that *woman is incapable of the same kind of activity as man*. But now the whole woman movement has for a long time been emphasising the fact that woman is entitled, not only on her own behalf but more especially in her capacity as homekeeper, wife, and mother, to the full development of her powers and to equality with man in the family and in society. In the amaternal programme sketched above, however, the fanaticism, which charaterised the entire woman movement a generation ago, now evinces itself in the error that *equal rights* for the sexes must mean also *equal functions;* that the development of women's powers involves also their application in the same spheres of activity in which man is engaged; that *equality* of the sexes implies *sameness* of the sexes. While moderate feminism begins to see that, if man and wife compete, this rivalry can benefit[1] neither the woman, the man, nor the children, amaternal feminism urges the keenest competition. And if this is once accepted as advantageous to woman's personality and to society, then it is obvious that she must, with all the energy of the attacked, defend herself from the duties of maternity, because of which she would obviously come off second-best in the competition.

From the point of view of individualism it is obvious that the *law* must set no limitations to woman's practice of a vocation, unless evident hygienic dangers menace either her or the coming generation. Women must, for their own sake as well as for that of society, have free *choice of work*, for life and nature possess innumerable unforeseen possibilities. Nevertheless, it does happen that a woman who gives superior children to humanity may, nevertheless, feel herself incapable of educat-

---

[1] It can even be shown that, if man invades the so-called woman's spheres (for example the art of cooking or of dressmaking), it is most frequently he who makes new discoveries and attains great success!

ing them; likewise it sometimes happens that a husband and wife who have exceptional children, cannot endure to live together. In neither case has law or custom a right to force upon a mother or a father a yoke that is intolerable or to demand of a mother or a father unreasonable sacrifices.

But the right to limit the choice of work, the law does not possess; nature assumes that right herself: first of all from the axiom that no one can be in two places at the same time, and in the second place because no one can respond simultaneously and with full energy to two different spiritual activities. One cannot, for example, count even to one hundred and at a certain number give a simple grasp of the hand without suspending the counting momentarily. Although no one has ever been denied the privilege of solving a mathematical problem and of following carefully at the same time a piece of music, yet it is certain that the effectiveness of both intellectual activities would be thereby diminished. These extremely simple observations can be continued until the most complex are reached. If the observation be directed to the sphere of domestic life, every wife and mother who *is willing to institute impartial observations of self*, will affirm the difficulty of working with a divided mind.

If a mother carries on her work at home and must put it away in order to be beside the sick-bed of her child, or to make those arrangements which assure domestic comfort, or to help her husband, then she feels that her book or her picture suffers, that the activity which binds her more intimately to the home relaxes for a time the intimacy of her connection with her work. One can by day carry on a dull industrial task, and by night produce an achievement of the soul; but one cannot let one's soul radiate in one direction without impairing its energy in another. A work needs exclusive devotion. And this is, viewed externally, difficult to attain in joint action; viewed from within, it requires a renunciation that in the case of a loving soul evokes a continual inner struggle. For that reason, also, literature with woman as its subject has for some decades been filled with the great conflict of modern woman's life: the conflict between vocation and parents, between vocation and husband, between vocation and child. Certainly the family has often been a torture chamber for individuality, as a consequence of laws and customs, which the future will regard as we now do the rack and the thumbscrew. But nature is more severe than law and custom when she confronts us with a choice which, however it may turn out, tears a piece from our heart.

And now neither custom nor man demands of woman the "sacrifice of the personality." This sacrifice is required only by the law of limitations which rules over us all.

The creative man or the man working objectively must often condemn the emotional side of his personality to a partial development; he must for the sake of his work renounce many family values important for this emotional side of his being. Even if shorter working hours could partially diminish this cultural offering, the *inner* conflict, for the man or the woman, is not settled thereby.

Even if a man, in the consciousness of his wife's endowment of talent, assumed a number of domestic duties, especially those pertaining to the children, the inner conflict would still continue. And this conflict is in no way solved by the amaternal theory that the personal life must be placed above the instinct life. For, as has been emphasised, the choice is not between the personal and the instinct life, but between the intellectual and the emotional side of woman's personality. And the solution of this choice has not been discovered by the amaternals, who would combine commercial work with marriage and maternity. Women who remain unmarried or who give up commercial activity which they cannot carry on in the home, have not *settled the conflict either*, but have only reduced its difficulties.

The fundamental error of the amaternal solution of the problem is that it characterises motherliness as a *non-social* instinct, but, on the other hand, defines the "personal" activity of woman as an expression of the social instinct. *For all social instincts have been developed by culture out of primitive instincts*. All cultural development lies between the sex impulse of the Australian negress and the erotic sentiment of Elizabeth Barrett

Browning's sonnets. And when the amaternals assert that motherliness, which "we have in common with beasts and savages," cannot be an expression of the personality, their argument has the same validity as that which would deny to the Sistine Chapel the quality of an expression of personality because beasts and savages also exhibit the decorative instinct.

The development of the mother instinct into motherliness is one of the greatest achievements in the progress of culture, a development by which the maternal functions have continually become more complex and differentiated. Already in the case of the higher animals maternity involves much more than the mere act of giving birth; an animal not only faces death for her young, she gives them also a training which often indicates power of judgment. A cat, for instance, which sought in vain to prevent her kitten from entering the water and which finally threw the kitten in and then pulled it out, thus obtaining the desired result of her pedagogy, had not, as have so many modern mothers, read Spencer, but could, nevertheless, put many of these mothers to shame. Even the initial maternal functions, nursing and physical care, involve a culture of the spiritual life of the mother, not only through an increase in tenderness, but also in observation, discrimination, judgment, self-control; a woman's character often develops more in a month during which she is occupied with the care of children, than in years of professional work. Mother love and the reciprocal love which it awakens in the child, not only exercise the first deep influence upon the individual's life of feeling, but this love is *the first form of the law of mutual help—it is the root of altruism, the cotyledon* of a now widely ramified tree of "social instincts."

Although woman through the mere *physical* functions of motherhood makes a great social contribution, the importance of her contribution is greatly enhanced if one also takes into consideration her *spiritual* nature. And notwithstanding the fact that fatherhood has also, to a certain degree, developed in man the qualities of tenderness, watchfulness, patience, yet the enormous predominance of woman's *physical* share in parenthood, in comparison with man's, is in itself enough to create, in course of time, the intimate connection which still exists to-day between mother and child, as well as the difference between the personality of woman and man. The physical functions of motherhood were the fundamental reasons for the earliest division of labour. And this division of labour, the aim of which, next to self-preservation, was for both sexes the protection of posterity, augmented and strengthened the qualities which each sex employed for its special functions. All human qualities lie latent in each. But they have been so specialised by this division of labour, or, on the other hand, suppressed by it, that they now appear in varying proportions: in woman, a careful, managing, supervising, lifeguarding, inward-directed sense of love; in man, courage, desire for action, force of will, power of thought, an activity subduing nature and life, became the distinguishing characteristics; and fatherhood became psychologically, as it is physiologically, something different from motherhood. Even if culture continues to efface the sharp lines of demarcation, so that it becomes more and more impossible to generalise about "woman" and "man," and increasingly more necessary for each and every woman to solve the "woman question" individually, yet from the point of view of the race, the *division of labour must on the whole remain the same as that which hitherto existed*, if the higher development of mankind shall continue in uninterrupted advance to more perfect forms. It is necessary for *these higher ends of culture* that woman *in an ever more perfect manner shall fulfil what has hitherto been her most exalted task:* the bearing and rearing of the new generation.

The amaternal assertion, that motherliness can be no higher than justice and truth, is an infuriating antithesis. It is as if one should assert that "air is better than water, or both better than bread." Both assertions place the fundamental condition of life counter to other needs of life! Who shall exercise justice and truth when no new men are born? And, moreover, how shall justice and truth increase in mankind if children are not trained to a greater reverence for justice and a deeper love of truth? In order to fulfil this one office *of education* well, mothers need their *universal human culture in its entirety.* But even if this were not so, if motherhood did not require the concentration of woman's personality; even if motherliness remained only "primitive instinct," yet this instinct, in the women who have guarded it, is more valuable for mankind than the universal human development of power of the women who have lost this instinct. No social nor individual activity of women could compensate for the extinction of this "instinct," which only recently in Messina drove hundreds of mothers to shield their children with their own bodies; this "instinct," which recently impelled a mother, who learned before she gave birth to her child that her own life must be the price for the saving of that of the child, to cry: "I have lived, but the life of my child belongs now to mankind—save the child!" So the mother died without even having seen the beautiful being for whom she gave her life. In the world of "personally" developed women, however, after a new Messina catastrophe the mothers would be found with their manuscript and their pictures in their arms. And confronted with a choice like that related above, the mother would answer: "Let the child die, I will live my personal life to the end."

The amaternal type must persist for the present. There are in reality in our time many women who with unresponsive eyes can pass by a lovely child, among them even mothers who do not feel the pure sensuousness, the wise madness, the intoxicating delight which such a child awakens in every motherly woman; mothers who have no conception what a fascinating subject for study the soul of a child can offer. Jean Paul, who scourged worthless mothers and tried to awaken the repressed maternal instinct of his time with the charge that a woman who is bored when she has children, is a contemptible creature, would find to-day many mothers who are bored only if they have their children about them.

And these cerebral, amaternal women must obviously be accorded the freedom of finding the domestic life, with its limited but intensive exercise of power meagre, beside the feeling of power which they enjoy as public personalities, as consummate women of the world, as talented professionals. But they have not the right to *falsify life values* in their own favour so that they themselves shall represent the highest form of life, the "human personality" in comparison with which the "instinctively feminine" signifies a lower stage of development, a poorer type of life.

Women who have produced books and works of art, to be compared, as respects permanence of value, to confetti at a carnival, have, according to this viewpoint, proved themselves human individualities, while a mother who has contributed an endless amount of clear thought, rich understanding, warm feeling, and strong will to the education of a fine group of children, requires a public office in order to prove herself a "human personality"! The brain work which a woman employs in a commercial concern bears witness to her individuality, but the brain work which a large, well-managed household demands, does not. The woman physician who delivers a mother expresses her "personality," but the mother has put no "personality" into the feelings with which she has borne the child, the dreams with which she has consecrated it, the ideas in accordance with which she has educated it! The girl who has passed her examinations has proved herself a developed human being; but her grandmother, who is now filled with the kindness and wisdom which she has won in a life dedicated to domestic duties, a life in which the restricted sphere of her duties did not prevent the comprehensiveness of her cultural interests, nor her all-embracing sympathy with humanity—such a woman is not a personality!

When men advance as an argument against women's rights the fear that women will lose their womanliness in public life, the older feminists answer that womanliness, especially motherliness, is rooted too firmly in nature to make it possible for this danger to exist. Nothing has, however, become more clear in this amaternalistic time than that motherliness is *not* an indestructible instinct. Just as our time produces in increasing numbers sterile women and women incapable of nursing their children, so it produces more and more psychically amaternal women. We can pass in silence the cases of children martyred in families or in children's homes, for sexual perversity and religious fanaticism often play a rôle in such connections; we can also pass by the millions of mothers who bring about the abortion of their offspring, for the poor are driven to such practices largely by necessity, the rich mostly by love of pleasure. There still remain a sufficient number of women in whom the mother instinct has faded away because of a course of thought like that just described. Our time furnishes manifold proofs of the fact that the mother instinct can easily be weakened, or even entirely disappear, although the erotic impulse continues to live; that motherliness is not a spontaneous natural instinct, but the product of thousands of years not merely of *child-bearing*, but also of *child-rearing;* and that it must be strengthened in each new generation by the personal care which mothers bestow upon their children. A woman learns to love the strange child whom she nurses as if it were her own; a father who can devote himself to the care of his little children is possessed by an almost "motherly tenderness" for them, as are also older brothers and sisters for the little ones whom they care for. But while those who advocate the cause of the amaternal women draw from such facts the conclusion that motherliness cannot be used as a criterion of womanliness, yet an entirely different conclusion forces itself upon everyone who sees in the united uplift of the individual and of mankind the criterion of the life-enhancing effect of the woman movement, the conclusion that the amaternal soul not only confirms the worst apprehensions of men in regard to the results of the woman movement, but also constitutes the greatest danger to the woman movement itself. For the amaternal ideas will evoke a violent reaction *on the part of men*, in case such a reaction does not appear at an early stage on the part of women.

This latter reaction might also include a rebellion against the methods of industrial production, which exhaust the strength of mothers and children. For the objection of industrialism, that "it cannot exist without women," falls to the ground in face of the fact that a race cannot exist without sound and moral mothers. And "moral" means, here, mothers capable and willing to bear sound children and to train children along moral lines. If, on the contrary, Europe and America adhere to the economic and ethical principles which prevent a number of able and willing women of this type from becoming mothers, and if numbers of other women who could be mothers continue unwilling to assume the burden of motherhood, then this problem will finally become the problem of *a future for the European–American people*.

The woman movement must now with resolute determination abandon the narrow, biased attitude, psychologically natural a generation ago when the zealots of feminism had no other standard of value for an idea, an investigation, or a book, than whether they *advanced or did not advance* the cause of woman; whether they *proved or did not prove* woman's equality with man. For woman's work, studies, and other accomplishments, no other standard was applied than that of equality with man's work, man's studies, and the accomplishments of man. In a word, the proposition was that woman should be enabled to perform at the same time the life-work of a woman and of a man!

It is through these hybrids that the feminine sex transgresses against the masculine. And this is one reason why our time is so filled with the tragic vicissitudes of women. Truly, every progressive person must agree with Goethe's aphorism, "I love him whom the impossible lures." For, thus allured, man has elevated his particular generation above the generation preceding. But *in action* every one must go down who is not imbued with the consciousness that whoever exceeds his limits is liable to tragic consequences, in the modern psychological view of the guilt attaching to one who undertakes more than his strength will allow.

. . . .

But our time exhibits also other less convulsively strained conditions of the feminine soul and therefore also brighter fates for woman. It shows not infrequently wives united with their husbands, not only by the sympathy which the human personality of each inspires, but also by the erotic attraction which the sex character of each exercises. And they have both won thereby that unity through which all the best and highest powers of their being are liberated and elevated as by religion. And their parenthood will then be the highest expression of this religion.

Only religious natures are—in the deepest meaning of the word—loving or faithful or creative. It is the same soul which in one person reveals itself in ecstasy of belief, in a second in ardour of creation, in a third in a great erotic passion, in the fourth as parental love, in others again as love of country, as enthusiasm for freedom, desire for reform. At times one and the same soul, a woman's or a man's, is kindled by all these passions. But never has the same soul been able *at the same time* to feed all these passions in their highest potency. Whether it be God, a work, or a human being that the soul embraces with its entire devotion, the religious character of this devotion always evinces itself in increasing longing, an endless susceptibility, a more persistent search after means of expression, a continual service, an inexhaustible patience in waiting for reciprocal activity from the object of love. The religious strength of a feeling consists in this, that the soul in every work, every sorrow, every joy,—in a word, in every spiritual condition, every experience,—is, consciously as well as unconsciously, more closely united with God, with the work, with the beloved, until every finest fibre of one's being reaches down to the profound depths which the object of love represents for the lover.

In this necessary condition of concentration of the spiritual life is found the truth of woman's complaint that the man, absorbed by his work, "no longer loves her"; the truth of the experience that earthly love indisputably detracts from the love of God; the truth of the frequent experience of husband and wife that with children the wealth of their spiritual life together is in certain respects inevitably diminished; the truth of man's fear that woman's absorption in a life-work personally dear to her must to a certain degree detract from her devotion to the home; the truth of the experience that the office of mother often interferes with the development of woman's intellectual power.

Only persons who distinguish themselves by what Heine called "exuberance of mental poverty," or what I might call analogously an "abyss of superficiality," have not experienced the severe and beautiful psychic truth of Jesus' glorification of *simplicity*. The quiet harkening to the voice of God or to the inspiration of work or to the delicate vibrations of another soul, which daily, hourly, momentarily, are the conditions that enable the soul to live wholly in its belief, its work, its love, so that these feelings may grow stronger and the soul grow greater through these feelings—all this has "simplicity" as a condition; in a word, symmetrical unity, longing for completeness, inner poise, the swift emotion. Fidelity—to a belief, a work, a love—is no product of duty. It is a process of growth.

These are the conditions to which many modern women, womanly at heart but divided, restless, groping, attempting much, will not submit. They could even learn to reverence these conditions in the child for whom play is such sacred seriousness; but instead they transform the most sacred earnest into play.

Other women, on the contrary, are beginning to understand these conditions of growth and to comprehend that it was exactly the protected position of woman in the home, which has made it possible for her family feeling to acquire that depth which is to be attained only by concentration. But if this is no longer possible, then woman will love those that belong to her with less religious warmth. Nothing can better illustrate the difference still existing between man and woman in this respect, than the fact that most men would consider themselves unfortunate if their entire exercise of power were concentrated upon the family, while most women still feel themselves fortunate when they have been given the opportunity to exercise to the uttermost the tendency inherent in them. For most women love best *personally* and *in propinquity*, while the potency of love in man often seeks distant goals. Woman is happy in the degree to which she can bestow her love upon a person closely connected with her; if she cannot do that, then she may be useful, resigned, content, but never happy.[1] The very fact that woman's strongest *primitive instinct* coincided with her *greatest* cultural *office* has been an essential factor in the harmony of her being.

The modern developed mother feels with every breath a grateful joy in that she lives the most perfect life when she can contribute her developed human powers, her liberated human personality, to the establishment of a home and to the vocation of motherhood. These functions conceived and understood as social, in the embracing sense in which the word is now used, give the new mother a richer opportunity to exercise her entire personality than she could find in modern commercial work. In one such occupation she must suppress either the intellectual or the emotional side of her nature; in another, the life either of the imagination or of the will. In domestic duties, on the contrary, these powers of the soul can work in unison. This is undoubtedly the deepest reason why, taken as a whole, women have become more harmonious, and men stronger in any special crisis, women more soulful, men more gifted. On this account men offer their great sacrifice more readily for an idea, or for the accomplishment of a work; women, for persons closely connected

[1] The best proof of this is that many women who, in a life free from care in an outward sense, were comparable only to geese or peacocks, nevertheless, when hard times came and gave them opportunity to develop their power of love, not only proved themselves heroines, but asserted that their "happy" years were those in which they had so "sacrificed" themselves.

with them. And yet this co-operation of woman's spiritual powers was in earlier times partly repressed by man's demand for passivity on the part of woman as a thinking and willing personality, but for her unceasing activity as promoter of his comfort and that of the entire home. The mother of to-day can, on the contrary, exercise, as distributer, her culture, her thought, her supervision, her judgment, and her criticism, in order to make fully effective the faculty of her sex for foresight and organisation. She applies a great amount of spiritual energy to the selection of the essentials and the subordination of secondary things, to the creation of such facilities in the material work that time and means are left for the spiritual values, which, alas, are still neglected in the domestic economy of small, private households, as well as in national housekeeping. And as mother, modern woman is offered the first fitting opportunity to assert herself as a thinking and willing personality.

The significance of the vocation of mother has been underrated in its significance even by moderate feminists. But these were right when they demonstrated that the "sanctity" of this office had become a mere phrase, so badly or amateurishly was this vocation fulfilled—an indictment in which Nietzsche and feminism for one rare moment are on common ground. Mothers needed the spur of this contempt; it was necessary that their feeling of responsibility, their universal human culture, their personal self-reliance, should be aroused by the woman movement. Only so could the new generation acquire the new type of women who for the present seek to qualify themselves by self-culture for the office of mother, in the expectation that for all women an obligatory education for motherhood will be realised. So long as this vocation *can* be practised without any training, nothing can be known of the possibilities whereby ordinary mothers may become good educators—unless they place the mother love and the intuitive understanding of the nature of the child that it affords above even the best outside teachers. Just as a glorious voice makes a country girl a "natural singer," so nature has at all times made certain mothers—and not least the women of the people—natural educators of children.

The biography of nearly every great man shows the place the mother through her personality occupied in the life of her son, the atmosphere which she diffused about her in the home, her direct and indirect influence. But only the culture of their natural gifts with conscious purpose will make of mothers artists.

When Nietzsche wrote: "*There will come a time when we shall have no other thought than education,*" and when he placed this education specifically in the hands of mothers, least of all did he mean those "arts of education," from which amaternals believe they "guard" children by rejecting an "artistically creative" home training by the mother, as a violence to the peculiar characteristic of the child!

The *new mother*, as the doctrine of evolution and the true woman movement have created her, stands with deep veneration before the mystic depths she calls her child, a being in whom the whole life of mankind is garnered. The richer the nature of the child is, the more zealously she endeavours to preserve for him that simplicity which he needs, and at the same time to provide for him the material that will enable him to work for himself. She insures to the child the pleasures adapted to his age, pleasures which at no later time can be enjoyed so intensely. The effect upon him of his playfellows and books, of nature, art, music, conversation, of the entire home *milieu* which the child receives, above all the influence of the personality and interests of the father and mother—all these the mother who is an artist in education observes in order to learn the natural proclivity of the child and then *directly to strengthen and encourage* it. At the same time she endeavours to find out what *restraints* are necessary *in order that the natural bent be not impeded in its growth by secondary qualities*. But the new type of mother does not seek to *eradicate;* she recognises the likeness between wheat and tares. The Christian education, which has thus far prevailed, has exercised a restraining oppression or has done violence to the "sinful nature," which must be broken and bent; this education was dermatological, not psychological, in method.

The new mother is especially characterised by the fact that she has rejected this earlier method. She allows her child, within certain bounds, full freedom, and demands, beyond those bounds, unconditional obedience. She helps the child to find for himself ever nobler motives for repression. This she can do because from the very beginning she has taken care of him; year by year she has persevered in the effort to establish good habits; she has tried to enlist as aids, food, bath, bed, dress, air, and play in the effort to keep him strong, sound, sexually pure—conditions fundamental to the whole later conduct of life. Such a methodical physical care *can* be performed by the mother herself, while, on the other hand, in the first years of childhood paid hands might, through carelessness, stupidity, cruelty, laxity, or over-indulgence, destroy the glorious possibilities. If the prevention of *the possibilities of nature being warped or destroyed* constituted all that a mother could give, this one task would, nevertheless, be more important than any social relief work.

What characterises the new mother is that she understands the enormous significance of the *first years*, when the indispensable "training" takes place, in which the future life of the child is determined by the methods employed—whether they be those of torture or of culture, irrational or rational. Then the great problem must be solved of establishing willing obedience from within in place of the hitherto *enforced* obedience from without; of maintaining self-control, won by self, in place of self-control *imposed* from without; of evoking voluntary renunciation in place of enforcing renunciation. For the capacity for obedience, for self-control, for renunciation, is one of the qualities fundamental to the whole later conduct of life. The new mother knows this as well as the mother of former times. But she endeavours to create this capacity by slow and sure means. The same thing obtains in regard to physical and psychical courage, which in the early years can often be so demoralised by fright that it can never emerge again. The training which hitherto was customary—based on *compelling* and *forbidding*—had its effect only upon the surface and *prevented* the child from experiencing *the results of his own choice.*

It is this *indirect* education by results which is the new mother's method. Her unceasing vigilance and consistency are required in order that the child shall actually bear the results of his actions. What she needs for this is first and foremost, *time, time,* and again *time*. Apparently good effects can be obtained much quicker by intervening, preventing, punishing, but thus are turned aside the *real* results. By this method the child is deprived of the *inner* growth, which only the fully experienced reality with its components of bitter and sweet can give; and this growth the new mother endeavours to advance. Much more time still is necessary to play the psychological game of chess, which consists in the checkmating of black by white; in other words, the conquest of negative characteristics by positive, through the child's own activity—a task in which the child at first must be guided, just as in the assimilation of the elements of every other accomplishment, but in which he can later perfect himself. Modern investigation in the realm of the soul enables us to see the dangers which sometime will demand quite as new methods in spiritual hygiene as bacteriology has created in the hygiene of the body. But we still leave unexercised powers of the soul, still misunderstand spiritual laws which sometime will radically transform the means of education. At some future day the new mothers will institute legal protection for children to an extent incomprehensible to us and therefore provocative only of smiles. For example, legal prohibition of corporal punishment by parents as well as teachers; legal prohibition of child labour, of certain tenement conditions, certain "amusements," certain improper uses of the press. For the present every individual educator must *set these laws over himself;* must sedulously create counter influences to cope with the destructive influences which great cities, especially, exert upon children.[1] The new

[1] How many children have had their idea of right debased by the manner in which the "Captain of Köpernick" was received at his liberation—to cite only one example.

mothers lead children out into nature and endeavour to satisfy their zeal for activity by appropriate tasks as well as to encourage by suitable means their love of invention and their impulse for play. In the country children provide much for themselves. But what both city and country children need is a mother familiar with nature, who can answer the questions which the child is by his own observations prompted to ask; and the number of such mothers is continually increasing. Both city and country children need also a mother who can tell stories. Just as the settlement gardens most clearly demonstrate how sundered the working people of the great cities are from nature, so the "story evenings," which are now established for children, show how far children have been permitted to stray from the mother, who formerly gathered them about her for the hour of story, play, and song. What, finally, children need is the mother's delicate revelation of the sexual "mystery," which often early exercises the thoughts of the child and in which he should be initiated quietly and gradually by the mother.

All the educational influences here outlined emanate not only from the enlightened, exceptional mother; they are exercised by the average mother of to-day to better advantage than by the spiritually significant mother of fifty years ago. And they are *quite as essential*, in order that the highest possibility within the reach of each may be attained, in the education of the genius as in that of the ordinary child. Such influences in like degree strengthen the innate bent of the genius and raise the average, from generation to generation, to a level where man can live according to higher standards than those of the present time. The new mothers understand that for the utilisation of all these opportunities that make their appearance in the first seven years of the child's life, their motherly tenderness, gentleness, and patience do not suffice; that they need in addition all the intelligence, imagination, fine feeling, scientific methods of observation, ethical and æsthetic culture and other spiritual acquisitions they possess, as direct and indirect fruits of the woman movement.

When student and comrade life begin to claim the children, when the influence of the mother—that is of the new mother who has respect for the peculiar characteristic, the human worth, and the right of the child to live his own life—becomes more indirect, she nevertheless bears in mind that it is of the utmost importance that the son and the daughter should *find the mother*, when they return to the parental roof; that they should be able to breathe there an atmosphere of peace and warmth; that they should find the attentive eye, the listening ear, the helpful hand; that the mother should have the repose, the fine feeling, the observation requisite for following, without interfering with, the conflicts of youth; that she should not demand confidences but be always at hand to receive them; that she should show vital sympathy for the plans of work, the disappointments, the joys, of the young people; that she should always have time for caresses, tears, smiles, comfort, and care; that she should divine their moods, and anticipate their desires. By all these means the mother perpetuates in the soul of the child, unknown to him and to herself, her own personality. The talent which she has not redeemed by a productive work of her own, perhaps often for that very reason, benefits mankind in a son or a daughter, in whose soul the mother has implanted the social ideas, the dreams, the rebellion, which later become in them social deeds or works of art. Above all, in the restless, sensitive, life-deciding years when the boy is becoming a youth and the little girl a maiden, the mother needs quiet and leisure to be able to give the ineffably needy children "the hoarded, secret treasure of her heart," as the beautiful saying of Dürer runs.

When such a mother is found, and such mothers are already found, she is the most splendid fruit of the woman movement's sowing upon the field of woman's nature.

Because the new mother created for herself an open space about her own personality, she understands her son or her daughter when they in their turn push her aside in order to create that same open space about themselves. For in every generation the young renounce the ideals and the aims of their parents. The knowledge of this does not prevent the new mother, any more than it did the mother of earlier times, from feeling the pain incident to being set aside. But the former looks forward to a day when the son and daughter will freely choose her as a friend, having discovered what a significant pleasure the mother's personality can afford them.

As the bird's nest is made of nothing but bits of straw and down, so the feeling of home is fashioned out of soft, simple things; out of little activities that are neither ponderable nor measurably as political or as economic factors. When Segantini painted the two nuns looking wistfully into the bird's nest, he gave expression to the deepest pain that many modern women experience, the pain resulting from the consciousness that their life, notwithstanding its freedom, is lonely, because it has denied them the privilege of making a home and as a consequence has failed to afford them the joy of creation, which nature intended they should have, and of continuity of life in children to whom they gave birth.

Here we stand at a point where the woman movement parallels the other social revolutions, undeviatingly as the rails of a track, and leads to the same objective. Modern men and women, and especially women, have forfeited an opportunity for happiness in the loss of the feeling of homogeneity and security. Just as formerly the property-holding family felt a secure sense of proprietorship in the ancestral estate, so every member of the home group felt himself safe in the family. Now the children cannot depend with certainty upon the parents, nor the parents upon the children; the wife upon the husband, nor the husband upon the wife. Each in extremity relies only upon himself. The character of man is thus altered quite as much as trees are changed when they are left standing alone in the denuded forest of which they once formed a part. If they can withstand the storms, they have produced more "character" than they had when they stood close together, under a mutual protection that nevertheless enforced uniformity.

From their earliest youth innumerable women must now care for themselves, as well as decide for themselves. Thus the feeling of independence of modern woman has increased through the sacrifice of her peace; her individual characteristics, at the expense of her harmony. Her feeling of loneliness is mitigated to a certain degree by the growing feeling of community with the whole. But this feeling cannot compensate certain natures for the forfeiture of the advantages which women of earlier times possessed, when they sat secure and protected within the four walls of the home, sucked the juice from family chronicles, guarded family traditions, maintained the old holiday customs, lived at the same time in the past and in the present.

The new woman lives in the present, sometimes

even in the future—her land of romance! The enthusiasm of the old romanticism about a "hut and a heart" has little charm for her. For she knows reality and that prevents her from giving credence to the feminine illusion that twice two can be five. What she does know, on the contrary, is that out of fours she can gradually work out sixteen. While the women of former times could only save, the new woman can acquire. Woman's beautiful, foolish superstition regarding life has vanished, but her eagerness to achieve can still remove mountains, her daring has still often the splendour of a dream. Intellectual values are for her no longer pastimes but necessities of life; with her culture has developed her feeling for truth and justice. This does not secure the new woman immunity at all times from new illusions and errors of feeling, nor does it prevent her developing passions whose value, to say the least, is questionable. But in and through her determination "to be some one," to have a characteristic personality, she has acquired a love of life, in its diverse manifestations, both good and evil; a new capacity to enjoy her own and others' individuality, as well as a new joy—sometimes an unblushing, insolent joy—in expressing her own being. In place of the earlier resignation toward society, the expression of rebellion is found even in the sparkling eye of the school-girl, with red cap upon her curly hair.

The young women of to-day, married or single,

mothers as well as those who are childless, are still more vigorous in soul, more courageous, more eager for life than are men. Because all that which for men has so long been a matter of course, is for women new, rich, enchanting, comprising, as it does, free life in nature, scientific studies, serious artistic work economic independence. Even in a fine and soulful woman there is found something of the inevitable hardness toward herself and others of which an observer is instinctively conscious when he speaks of some woman as one who "will go far" upon the course she has chosen. The modern young woman desires above all else the elevation of her own personality. She experiences the same feeling of joy a man is conscious of when she realises that her strength of will is augmented, her ability becoming more certain, her depth of thought greater, her association of ideas richer. She stands ready to choose *her* work and follow *her* fate; in sorrow as in joy she experiences the blessedness of growth, and she loves her view of life and the work to which she has dedicated herself, often as devotedly as man loves his.

If we compare the seventeen-year-old girl of to-day with her progenitor living in the middle of the foregoing century, we find that the girl of earlier times was to a larger extent swayed by feeling, and that the modern girl is to a larger extent determined by ideas. The former was directed more to the centre of life, the latter remains often nearer the periphery; the former was warmer, the latter is more intelligent; the former was better balanced, the latter is more interesting.

The restlessness, the uncertainty, the feeling of emptiness, the suffering, that is sometimes experienced by the young woman of to-day, is primarily traceable to the disintegration of religious belief, which gave to the older generation of emancipated women an inner stability, resignation, and self-discipline. Scientific study has deprived many modern women of their belief and those who can create a new one, suited to their needs, are still very few. Thus to the outer homelessness an inner estrangement is added. The woman movement has, it is true, contributed indirectly to this spiritual distress by making the road to man's culture accessible to woman. For men also suffer in like manner, and suffer above all perhaps because our culture is unstable, aimless, and lacks style, owing to the very fact that it is at present without a religious centre. And even the future can give to mankind no such new centre as the Middle Ages had, for example, in Catholicism. The attainment of individualism has shut out that possibility forever.

But *one* factor in the religion of the past, the adoration of motherhood as divine mystery; *one* factor in the religion of the Middle Ages, the worship of the Madonna, has meanwhile been given back to the present by the doctrine of evolution, with that universal validity which the thought must possess which seeks to give again to culture a centre. Great, solitary individuals—prophets more often than sibyls—have proclaimed the religion of this generation. But the word will become flesh only when fathers and mothers instil into the blood and soul of children their devout hope for a higher humanity. When women are permeated by this hope, this new devout feeling, then they will recover the piety, the peace, and the harmony which for the present, and partly owing to feminism, have been lost.

The innumerable new relations which the woman movement has established between woman and the home, between woman and society, and all of the interchanges of new spiritual forces which have been put in operation because of these relations, cannot possibly take fixed form, at least not so long as the woman movement remains "a movement"; in other words, as long as everything is in a condition of flux, in a state of becoming, all spiritual relationships between individuals must change their form. Continual new, fine shades of feeling, not to be expressed in words, determine every woman's soul and every woman's fate. And even ancient feelings receive continually different nuances, different intonations. I am, therefore, laying down no laws but merely recapitulating certain suggestions based on what has previously been said in regard to the soul of the modern woman, as seen in that portion of the present generation whose age ranges between twenty and thirty years—that is to say, that part of the generation which is decisive for the immediate future.

Since co-education is becoming more and more general, each sex is beginning to have more esteem for the other, and woman, as well as man, is beginning to found self-respect upon work. When all women by culture and capacity for work have finally become strong-willed, self-supporting co-workers in society, then no woman will give or receive love for any extraneous benefit whatsoever. No outward tie and no outward gain through love—this is the ultimate aim of the new sex morale as the most highly developed modern young woman sees it.

The new woman is deeply convinced that the relation between the sexes attains its true beauty and sanctity only when every external privilege disappears on both sides, when man and woman stand wholly equal in what concerns their legal right and their personal freedom.

She demands that the contrasts between legal and illegal, rich and poor, boy and girl, shall disappear, and that society shall show the same interest in the complete human development of all children. She knows that when both sexes awake to a feeling of responsibility toward the future generation, then the real concern of sexual morale becomes the endeavor to give the race an ever more perfect progeny. And in order to feel in its fulness this command, maidens as well as youths must henceforth demand scientific instruction in sexual duties toward themselves and their possible children.

The new woman is also deeply convinced that only when she feels happy—and happiness signifies the development of the powers inherent in the personality—can she properly fulfil her duties as daughter, wife, and mother. She can consciously sacrifice a part of her personality, for example forego the development of a talent, but she can never subjugate nor surrender her whole personality and at the same time remain a strong-willed member of the family or of society, in the broadest meaning of the word. She must assert her conception of life, her feeling of right, her ideals. And no social considerations for children, husband, or family life are, for her, above the consideration which, in this respect, she owes to her own personality. When conflicts arise, she seeks, wherever possible, a solution that will permit her to fulfil her duty without annihilating herself. But if this is not possible, then she feels that it is her first duty not to fall below her ideal, either physically or spiritually. For this would prevent her from fulfilling precisely those duties for which she has so sacrificed herself; duties which she can perhaps perform later under other conditions, provided she has saved herself from being extinguished by brutality or despotism.

But along with this individualism there exists in the new woman a feeling for the unity of existence, the unity in which all things are parts and in which nothing is lost. She does not, then, look upon husband and children as continually demanding sacrifice and upon herself as being always sacrificed; she sees herself and them, as in the antiquity of the race, always existing *by means of one another*. She is not consumed by her love, for she knows that under such circumstances she would deprive her loved ones of the wealth of her personality. But although she will not, like the women of earlier times, abandon her ego *absolutely*, she will not, on the other hand, like certain modern feminists, keep it *unreservedly*. She will preserve upon a higher plane the old division of labour which made man the one who felled the game, fought the battles, made conquests, achieved advancement through victories; and which made woman the one who rendered the new domains habitable, who utilised the booty for herself and hers, who transmitted what was won to the new generation—all that of which woman's ancient tasks as guardian of the fire and cultivator of the fields are beautiful symbols. She feels that when each sex pursues its course for the happiness of the individual and of mankind, but at the same time and as an equal helps the other in the different tasks, then each is most capable, then society is most benefited.

The fact that there is still so much masculine brutality and despotism, and that there are so many legal means at man's disposal whereby he may put into practice with impunity this brutality and despotism, is the reason why the new woman is still always a "feminist," why she still maintains the fundamental tenets of the woman movement. But she is not a feminist in the sense that she turns *against* man. Her solution is always that of Mary Wollstonecraft: "We do not desire to rule over men but to rule over ourselves." She often exhibits now in deliberation and in determination the characteristics which were formerly called "masculine": practical knowledge, love of truth, courage of conviction; she desists more and more from unjust imputations and empty words; she proposes a greater number of well-considered suggestions for improvements. The woman movement has now in a word a more universally human, a less onesidedly feminine character. It emphasises more and more the fact that the right of woman is a necessity in order that she may fulfil her duties in the small, individual family, and exercise her powers in the great, universal human family for the general good. The new woman does not wish to displace man nor to abolish society. She wishes to be able to exercise *everywhere* her most beautiful prerogative to help, to support, to comfort. But this she cannot do so long as she is not free as a citizen and has not fully developed as a human personality. She knows that this is the condition not only of her own happiness, but also, in quite as high a degree, of the happiness of man. For every man who works, struggles, and suffers there is a mother, **a** wife, a sister, a daughter, who suffers with him. For every woman who in her way works and struggles, there is a father, a husband, a brother, or a son for whom her contribution directly or indirectly has significance. Above all, the modern woman understands that in every marriage wherein a wife still suffers under man's misuse of his legal authority, it is in the last analysis *the man who sustains the greatest injury*, for under present conditions he needs exercise neither kindness nor justice nor intelligence to be ruler in the family. These humane characteristics he must, therefore, begin to develop when the wife is legally his equal.

The sacred conviction of the new woman is that man and woman *rise together*, just as they *sink together*.

The antique sepulchres, on which man and wife stand hand in hand before the eternal farewell, could quite as well be the symbol of the entrance of modern man and modern woman into the new life, where they work together in order that the highest ideals of both—the ideals of justice and of human kindness—may assume form in reality. The motherly qualities of women are applied for the good of children as well as of the weak and the suffering. The arrival of the day when woman shall be given opportunity to exercise social motherliness in its full and popularly representative extent, can be only a question of time. In a century they will smile at our time, in which it was still the practice to debate about such obvious matters. And those who to-day ridicule the woman movement will be ridiculed most of all.

Then we shall attain such an outlook on the great forces of the time,—the emancipation movements of labouring men and of women,—that we shall see how necessary both were in order that society should come to understand that not the mass of material production, but the higher cultivation of the race is the social-political end, and that for this end the *service of mother* must receive the honour and oblation that the state now gives to *military service*.

And women themselves, whom nature has made creators and protectors of the tender life —the task for which nature even in the plant world has made such wonderful provision—will no longer resist being more intimately associated with nature, nearer to earth, more like plants, more restrained in outer sense and therefore, in inner respects, less active than man, who always had more of the freedom of movement of the forest animal. The woman of the future will not, as do many women of the present time, *wish to be freed from her sex;* but she will be freed from sexual hypertrophy, freed to *complete humanity*. For the universal, human characteristics, forced to *remain latent* in the primitive division of labour, because the father was obliged to exert all his strength in one direction and the mother in another, can now, through the facilities for culture in the struggle for existence, be developed on both sides: woman can develop the latent quality which became active in man as "manliness"; man can develop the latent quality which became active in woman as "womanliness." But the *proportional ratio* of these characteristics, which development has already strengthened, will *on the whole* remain fixed—the proportional ratio which, in the progress of evolution, gave to woman the ascendency in regard to inward creative powers, and to man the ascendency in regard to outward creative powers—a proportional ratio which for the present has made woman more gifted in the sphere of feeling, man more potent in the sphere of ideas; which has made her the listener and yearner in the sphere of the spiritual life, and him the pioneer investigator and founder of systems, that has given her more of the Christian, and him more of the pagan virtues. The improvement of the universal, human characteristics of both sexes elevates also the plane upon which they exercise their especial functions, valuable alike for culture. With increasing frequency the one sex may, when so desired, assume the culture function of the other.

A perfect fusion of the two spiritual sex-characters would, on the contrary, have the same result as physical hermaphroditism—sterility. Genius—and in using the term we limit its meaning to poetic genius, for real feminine genius has thus far appeared only in that domain—embraces, as emphasised above, both man and woman, but not harmoniously blended. For such a genius would be unproductive, as we imagine those celestial forms to be which are neither "man nor woman." The masculine and the feminine characteristics, which exist side by side in the poet soul, produce work in co-operation. Alternately, however, they seek to usurp the entire power, whereby is occasioned the disharmony which enters into the life of those who endeavour to fulfil at one and the same time the universal, human duties as well as those of sex. Indeed it may be that one of the reasons why great poetic geniuses, masculine as well as feminine, have often had no progeny at all, and in other cases one of little significance, is that their nature was not capable of a double production, that poetic creation received the richest part of their physical and psychical power.

Whether the opinion of genius expressed here is correct or not, does not, however, affect the general situation. For the genius will always go his own way, which is never that of the average man. From the point of view of the ordinary individual an effacement of the spiritual sex-character would be in still higher degree a misfortune for culture and nature. For it is the difference in the spiritual as well as in the physical sex-characteristics that makes love a fusion of two beings in a higher unity, where each finds the full deliverance and harmony of his being. With the elimination of the *spiritual* difference *psychical* love would vanish. There would be left, then, upon the one side, only the mating instinct, in which the same points of view as in animal breeding must obtain; on the other, only the same kind of sympathy which is expressed in the friendship between persons of the same sex, the sympathy in which the human, individual difference instead of sexual difference forms the attraction. In love, on the other hand, sympathy grows in intensity, the more universally human and at the same time sexually attractive the individual is: the "manly" in man is charmed by the "womanly" in woman, while the "womanly" in man is likewise captivated by the "manly" in woman, and *vice versa*. But when neither needs the *spiritual sex* of the other as his complement, then man, in erotic respects, returns to the antique conception of the sex relationship, of which Plato has drawn the final logical conclusion.

The "humanity" in the soul of man was strengthened when he felt himself necessary to mother and child. When woman by sweetness and tenderness taught man to love, not only to desire, then his humanity increased immeasurably.

In our time the average man is beginning to learn that woman does not desire him as man, that she looks down upon him as a lower kind of being, that she does not need him as supporter. He does not at all grasp what it is the woman of highest culture seeks, demands, and awaits from his sex. But he learns that even the mediocre woman rejects the best he has to give her erotically; that imbued as she is with ideals of "universal humanity," she no longer needs him as the supplement to her sexual being. Then brutality awakes in him anew; then his erotic life loses what humanity it had won; then he begins to hate woman. And not with the imaginative, theoretical hatred of thinkers and poets; but with the blind rage which the contempt of the weaker for the stronger arouses in him. And here we encounter what is, perhaps, the deepest reason for the present war between the sexes, appearing already in the literary world as well as in the labour market.

Here the extreme feminists play unconsciously about an abyss,—the depths in the nature of man out of which the elementary, hundred-thousand-year-old impulses arise, the impulses which all cultural acquisitions and influences cannot eradicate, so long as the human race continues to subsist and multiply under present conditions.

The feminism which has driven individualism to the point where the individual asserts her personality in opposition to, instead of within, the race; the individualism which becomes self-concentration, anti-social egoism, although the watchword inscribed upon its banner is "Society instead of the family,"—this feminism will bear the blame should the hatred referred to lead to war.

It would be a pity to conclude a survey of the influence of the woman movement with an expression of fear lest this extreme feminism should be victorious. I believe not; no more than I believe that the sun will for the present be extinguished or streams flow back to their sources.
No "culture" can annul the great fundamental laws of nature; it can only ennoble them; and motherhood is one of these fundamental laws. I hope that the future will furnish a new and a more secure protection for motherhood than the present family and social organisation affords. I place my trust in a new society, with a new morality, which will be a synthesis of the being of man and that of woman, of the demands of the individual and those of society, of the pagan and Christian conceptions of life, of the will of the future and reverence for the past.
When the earth blooms with this beautiful and vigorous flower of morality, there will no longer be a woman movement. But there will always be a woman question, not put by women to society but by society to women: the question whether they will continue in a higher degree to prove themselves worthy of the great privilege of being the mothers of the new generation.
In the degree in which this new ethics permeates mankind, women will answer this question in

life-affirmation. And the result of their life-affirmation will be an enormous enhancement of life, not only for women themselves but for all mankind.

THE END

A Selection from the Catalogue of

G. P. PUTNAM'S SONS

Complete Catalogue sent
on application

By Ellen Key

The Century of the Child

Cr. 8vo. With Frontispiece. Net, $1.50. By mail, $1.65

CONTENTS: The Right of the Child to Choose His Parents, The Unborn Race and Woman's Work, Education, Homelessness, Soul Murder in the Schools, The School of the Future, Religious Instruction, Child Labor and the Crimes of Children. This book has gone through more than twenty German Editions and has been published in several European countries.

"A powerful book."—*N. Y. Times.*

The Education of the Child

Reprinted from the Authorized American Edition of "The Century of the Child." With Introductory Note by EDWARD BOK.

Cr. 8vo. Net, 75 cents. By mail, 85 cents

"Nothing finer on the wise education of the child has ever been brought into print. To me this chapter is a perfect classic; it points the way straight for every parent, and it should find a place in every home in America where there is a child."—EDWARD BOK, Editor of the *Ladies' Home Journal.*

Love and Marriage

Cr. 8vo. Net, $1.50. By mail, $1.65

Ellen Key is gradually taking a hold upon the reading public of this country commensurate with the enlightenment of her views. In Europe and particularly in her own native Sweden her name holds an honored place as a representative of progressive thought.

New York G. P. Putnam's Sons London

Ellen Key
Her Life and Her Work
A Critical Study
By Louise Nystrom Hamilton

Translated by Anna E. B. Fries

12°. With Portrait

The name of Ellen Key has for years been a target for attacks of various kinds. Friends have in connection with the issues that have arisen in regard to the influence of her work become enemies and friction has been caused in many homes. Her ideals and her purposes have been misquoted and misinterpreted until the very convictions for which she stood have been twisted so as to appear to be the evils that she was attempting to combat. Her critics, not content with decrying and distorting the message that she had to give to the world, have even attacked her personal character; and as the majority of these had no direct knowledge in the matter, strange rumors and fancies have been spread abroad about her life. The readers of her books, who are now to be counted throughout the world by the hundreds of thousands, who desire to know the truth about this much discussed Swedish author, will be interested in this critical study by Louise Hamilton. The author is one who has been intimate with Ellen Key since her youth. She is herself the wife of the founder of the People's Hospital in Stockholm, where for over twenty years Ellen Key taught and lectured.

The volume gives an admirable survey of the purpose and character of Ellen Key's teachings and of her books.

New York   **G. P. Putnam's Sons**   London

"Packed with information about actual present-day business conditions and methods."
—REVIEW OF REVIEWS.

The American Business Woman

A Guide for the Investment, Preservation and Accumulation of Property, Containing Full Explanations and Illustrations of all Necessary Methods of Business

By

John Howard Cromwell, Ph.B., LL.B.

Counsellor-at-Law

Second Revised Edition. Octavo. 392 pages. $2.00 net. By mail, $2.20

"Mr. Cromwell's book is without doubt one of the valuable publications of the year . . . thoroughly well written and carefully thought out. . . . Fascinating as is the subject of mortgages, it is necessarily but one phase of the book. . . . The book, as before stated, is extremely valuable, and will be found a good investment, not only for women for whom it was primarily intended, but for many men."—*New York Times.*

G. P. Putnam's Sons
New York   London

"The most complete and compact study that has yet been made of the evolution of women's rights."—*N. Y. Evening Globe.*

A Short History of Women's Rights

From the days of Augustus to the Present Time

With Special Reference to England and the United States

By Eugene A. Hecker

Master in the Roxbury Latin School, Author of "The Teaching of Latin in Secondary Schools"

Crown 8vo. $1.50 net. (By mail, $1.65)

Mr. Hecker, an authoritative scholar, has set himself the task of telling the story of women's progress, and has done it with much painstaking and thoroughness, and with a manifestation of a high order of talent for discriminating as to materials and presenting them convincingly and interestingly. . . . One feels the studiousness of the author in every page. The matter presented is not only carefully arranged, but it is in a manner digested too; and thus the work becomes literature in a true sense, and not an unenlightened assembly of details and facts from the pages of the past.
—*St. Louis Times.*

G. P. Putnam's Sons
New York   London

Printed in the United States
126077LV00008B/55/A